The Antichrist

FRIEDRICH NIETZSCHE

GENERAL PRESS

Published by
GENERAL PRESS
4805/24, Fourth Floor, Krishna House
Ansari Road, Daryaganj, New Delhi - 110002
Ph : 011-23282971, 45795759
E-mail : generalpressindia@gmail.com

www.generalpress.in

First Edition : 2022

ISBN : 9789354993800

Published by Azeem Ahmad Khan for General Press

BESTSELLING NON-FICTION

- Annihilation of Caste by Dr B.R. Ambedkar
  Social Science, ISBN: 9789390492732
- Believe in Yourself by Joseph Murphy
  Self-Help/Motivational, ISBN: 9789388118385
- How I Made $2,000,000 in the Stock Market by Nicolas Darvas
  Self-Help, ISBN: 9789389716283
- How to Attract Money by Joseph Murphy
  Self-Help, ISBN: 9789388118408
- How to Enjoy Your Life and Your Job by Dale Carnegie
  Self-Help, ISBN: 9789387669017
- How to Stop Worrying and Start Living by Dale Carnegie
  Self-Help, ISBN: 9789380914817
- How to Win Friends and Influence People by Dale Carnegie
  Self-Help, ISBN: 9788180320217
- Jail Diary and Other Writings by Bhagat Singh
  Biographies & Memoirs, ISBN: 9789390492398
- Know Your Worth by NK Sondhi & Vibha Malhotra
  Self-Help/Motivational, ISBN: 9788180320231
- Meditations by Marcus Aurelius
  Philosophy, ISBN: 9789388118736
- My Experiments with Truth by Mahatma Gandhi
  Biographies & Memoirs, ISBN: 9789387669291
- My Inventions: The Autobiography of Nikola Tesla
  Biographies & Memoirs, ISBN: 9789388118132

Search the book by its ISBN

BESTSELLING NON-FICTION

- Relativity by Albert Einstein
  Science/Physics, ISBN: 9789380914220
- Reminiscences of a Stock Operator by Edwin Lefevre
  Business/Stock Market, ISBN: 9788194764816
- Success Through a Positive Mental Attitude by Napoleon Hill
  Self-Help, ISBN: 9789390492435
- The Art of War by Sun Tzu
  Self-Help, ISBN: 9789380914893
- The Autobiography of a Yogi by Paramahansa Yogananda
  Biographies & Memoirs, ISBN: 9789380914602
- The Diary of a Young Girl by Anne Frank
  Biographies & Memoirs, ISBN: 9789380914312
- The Elements of Style by William Strunk
  Non-Fiction, ISBN: 9789389157123
- The Law of Success by Napoleon Hill
  Self-Help, ISBN: 9788180320927
- The Power of Your Subconscious Mind by Joseph Murphy
  Self-Help, ISBN: 9788180320958
- The Richest Man in Babylon by George S. Clason
  Business & Economics, ISBN: 9789387669369
- The Science of Getting Rich by Wallace D. Wattles
  Self-Help, ISBN: 9788180320972
- The World as I See It by Albert Einstein
  Non-Fiction, ISBN: 9789388118125

Search the book by its ISBN

Contents

Introduction . . . 7

Preface . . . 27

The Antichrist . . . 29 - 120

Introduction

Save for his raucous, rhapsodical autobiography, "Ecce Homo," "The Antichrist" is the last thing that Nietzsche ever wrote, and so it may be accepted as a statement of some of his most salient ideas in their final form. Notes for it had been accumulating for years and it was to have constituted the first volume of his long-projected *magnum opus*, "The Will to Power." His full plan for this work, as originally drawn up, was as follows:

Vol.	I.	The Antichrist: An Attempt at a Criticism of Christianity.
Vol.	II.	The Free Spirit: A Criticism of Philosophy as a Nihilistic Movement.
Vol.	III.	The Immoralist: A Criticism of Morality, the Most Fatal Form of Ignorance.
Vol.	IV.	Dionysus: The Philosophy of Eternal Recurrence.

The first sketches for "The Will to Power" were made in 1884, soon after the publication of the first three parts of "Thus Spake Zarathustra," and thereafter, for four years, Nietzsche piled up notes. They were written at all the places he visited on his endless travels in search of health—at Nice, at Venice, at Sils-Maria in the Engadine (for long his favourite resort), at Cannobio, at Zürich, at Genoa, at Chur, at Leipzig. Several times his work was interrupted by other books, first by "Beyond Good and Evil," then by "The Genealogy of Morals" (written in twenty days), then by his Wagner pamphlets. Almost as often he changed his plan. Once he decided to expand "The Will to Power" to ten volumes, with "An Attempt at a New Interpretation of the World" as a general sub-title. Again he adopted the sub-title of "An Interpretation of All That Happens." Finally, he hit upon "An Attempt at a Transvaluation of All Values," and went back to four volumes, though with a number of changes in their arrangement. In September, 1888, he began actual work upon the first volume, and before the end of the month it was completed. The Summer had been one of almost hysterical creative activity. Since the middle of June he had written two other small books, "The Case of Wagner" and "The Twilight of the Idols," and before the end of the year he was destined to write "Ecce Homo." Sometime during December his health began to fail rapidly, and soon after the New Year he was helpless. Thereafter he wrote no more.

The Wagner diatribe and "The Twilight of the Idols" were published immediately, but "The Antichrist" did not get into type until 1895. I suspect that the delay was due to the influence of the philosopher's sister, Elisabeth Förster-Nietzsche, an intelligent and ardent but by no means uniformly judicious propagandist of his ideas. During his dark days of neglect and misunderstanding, when even family and friends kept aloof, Frau Förster-Nietzsche went with him farther than any other, but there were bounds beyond which she, also, hesitated to go, and those bounds were marked by crosses. One notes, in her biography of him—a useful but not always accurate work—an evident desire to purge him of the accusation of mocking at sacred things. He had, she says, great admiration for "the elevating effect of Christianity... upon the weak and ailing," and "a real liking for sincere, pious Christians," and "a tender love for the Founder of Christianity." All his wrath, she continues, was reserved for "St. Paul and his like," who perverted the Beatitudes, which Christ intended for the lowly only, into a universal religion which made war upon aristocratic values. Here, obviously, one is addressed by an interpreter who cannot forget that she is the daughter of a Lutheran pastor and the grand-daughter of two others; a touch of conscience gets into her reading of "The Antichrist." She even hints that the text may have been garbled, after the author's collapse, by some more sinister heretic. There is not the slightest reason to believe that any such garbling ever took place, nor is there any evidence that their common heritage of piety rested upon the brother as heavily as it rested upon the sister. On the contrary, it must be manifest that Nietzsche, in this book, intended to attack Christianity headlong and with all arms, that for all his rapid writing he put the utmost care into it, and that he wanted it to be printed exactly as it stands. The ideas in it were anything but new to him when he set them down. He had been developing them since the days of his beginning. You will find some of them, clearly recognizable, in the first book he ever wrote, "The Birth of Tragedy." You will find the most important of all of them—the conception of Christianity as *ressentiment*—set forth at length in the first part of "The Genealogy of Morals," published under his own supervision in 1887. And the rest are scattered through the whole vast mass of his notes, sometimes as mere questionings but often worked out very carefully. Moreover, let it not be forgotten that it was Wagner's yielding to Christian sentimentality in "Parsifal" that transformed Nietzsche from the first among his literary advocates into the most bitter of his opponents. He could forgive every other sort of mountebankery, but not that. "In me," he once said, "the Christianity of my forbears reaches its logical conclusion. In me the stern intellectual conscience that Christianity fosters and makes paramount turns *against* Christianity. In me Christianity... devours itself."

In truth, the present philippic is as necessary to the completeness of the whole of Nietzsche's system as the keystone is to the arch. All the curves of his speculation lead up to it. What he flung himself against, from beginning to end of his days of writing, was always, in the last analysis, Christianity in some form or other—Christianity as a system of practical ethics, Christianity as a political code, Christianity as meta physics, Christianity as a gauge of the truth. It would be difficult to think of any intellectual enterprise on his long list that did not, more or less directly and clearly, relate itself to this master enterprise of them all. It was as if his apostasy from the faith of his fathers, filling him with the fiery zeal of the convert, and particularly of the convert to heresy, had blinded him to every other element in the gigantic self-delusion of civilized man. The will to power was his answer to Christianity's affectation of humility and self-sacrifice; eternal recurrence was his mocking criticism of Christian optimism and millennialism; the superman was his candidate for the place of the Christian ideal of the "good" man, prudently abased before the throne of God. The things he chiefly argued for were anti-Christian things—the abandonment of the purely moral view of life, the rehabilitation of instinct, the dethronement of weakness and timidity as ideals, the renunciation of the whole hocus-pocus of dogmatic religion, the extermination of false aristocracies (of the priest, of the politician, of the plutocrat), the revival of the healthy, lordly "innocence" that was Greek. If he was anything in a word, Nietzsche was a Greek born two thousand years too late. His dreams were thoroughly Hellenic; his whole manner of thinking was Hellenic; his peculiar errors were Hellenic no less. But his Hellenism, I need not add, was anything but the pale neo-Platonism that has run like a thread through the thinking of the Western world since the days of the Christian Fathers. From Plato, to be sure, he got what all of us must get, but his real forefather was Heraclitus. It is in Heraclitus that one finds the germ of his primary view of the universe—a view, to wit, that sees it, not as moral phenomenon, but as mere aesthetic representation. The God that Nietzsche imagined, in the end, was not far from the God that such an artist as Joseph Conrad imagines—a supreme craftsman, ever experimenting, ever coming closer to an ideal balancing of lines and forces, and yet always failing to work out the final harmony.

The late war, awakening all the primitive racial fury of the Western nations, and there with all their ancient enthusiasm for religious taboos and sanctions, naturally focused attention upon Nietzsche, as upon the most daring and provocative of recent amateur theologians. The Germans, with their characteristic tendency to explain their every act in terms as realistic and unpleasant as possible, appear to have mauled him in a belated and unexpected embrace, to the horror, I daresay, of the Kaiser, and perhaps to the even greater horror of Nietzsche's own ghost. The folks of Anglo-Saxondom, with their equally characteristic tendency to explain all their enterprises romantically, simultaneously set him up as the Antichrist he no doubt secretly longed to be. The result was a great deal of misrepresentation and misunderstanding of him. From the pulpits of the allied countries, and particularly from those of England and the United States, a horde of patriotic ecclesiastics denounced him in extravagant terms as the author of all the horrors of the time, and in the newspapers, until the Kaiser was elected sole bugaboo, he shared the honors of that office with von Hindenburg, the Crown Prince, Capt. Boy-Ed, von Bernstorff and von Tirpitz. Most of this denunciation, of course, was frankly idiotic—the naïve pishposh of suburban Methodists, notoriety-seeking college professors, almost illiterate editorial writers, and other such numskulls. In much of it, including not a few official hymns of hate, Nietzsche was gravely discovered to be the teacher of such spokesmen of the extremest sort of German nationalism as von Bernhardi and von Treitschke—which was just as intelligent as making George Bernard Shaw the mentor of Lloyd-George. In other solemn pronunciamentoes he was credited with being philosophically responsible for various imaginary crimes of the enemy—the wholesale slaughter or mutilation of prisoners of war, the deliberate burning down of Red Cross hospitals, the utilization of the corpses of the slain for soap-making. I amused myself, in those gaudy days, by collecting newspaper clippings to this general effect, and later on I shall probably publish a digest of them, as a contribution to the study of war hysteria. The thing went to unbelievable lengths. On the strength of the fact that I had published a book on Nietzsche in 1906, six years after his death, I was called upon by agents of the Department of Justice, elaborately outfitted with badges, to meet the charge that I was an intimate associate and agent of "the German monster, Nietzsky." I quote the official *procès verbal*, an indignant but often misspelled document. Alas, poor Nietzsche! After all his laborious efforts to prove that he was not a German, but a Pole—even after his heroic readiness, via anti-anti-Semitism, to meet the deduction that, if a Pole, then probably also a Jew!

But under all this alarmed and preposterous tosh there was at least a sound instinct, and that was the instinct which recognized

Nietzsche as the most eloquent, pertinacious and effective of all the critics of the philosophy to which the Allies against Germany stood committed, and on the strength of which, at all events in theory, the United States had engaged itself in the war. He was not, in point of fact, involved with the visible enemy, save in remote and transient ways; the German, officially, remained the most ardent of Christians during the war and became a democrat at its close. But he was plainly a foe of democracy in all its forms, political, religious and epistemological, and what is worse, his opposition was set forth in terms that were not only extraordinarily penetrating and devastating, but also uncommonly offensive. It was thus quite natural that he should have aroused a degree of indignation verging upon the pathological in the two countries that had planted themselves upon the democratic platform most boldly, and that felt it most shaky, one may add, under their feet. I daresay that Nietzsche, had he been alive, would have got a lot of satisfaction out of the execration thus heaped upon him, not only because, being a vain fellow, he enjoyed execration as a tribute to his general singularity, and hence to his superiority, but also and more importantly because, being no mean psychologist, he would have recognized the disconcerting doubts underlying it. If Nietzsche's criticism of democracy were as ignorant and empty, say, as the average evangelical clergyman's criticism of Darwin's hypothesis of natural selection, then the advocates of democracy could afford to dismiss it as loftily as the Darwinians dismiss the blather of the holy clerks. And if his attack upon Christianity were mere sound and fury, signifying nothing, then there would be no call for anathemas from the sacred desk. But these onslaughts, in point of fact, have behind them a tremendous learning and a great deal of point and plausibility—there are, in brief, bullets in the gun, teeth in the tiger,—and so it is no wonder that they excite the ire of men who hold, as a primary article of belief, that their acceptance would destroy civilization, darken the sun, and bring Jahveh to sobs upon His Throne.

But in all this justifiable fear, of course, there remains a false assumption, and that is the assumption that Nietzsche proposed to destroy Christianity altogether, and so rob the plain people of the world of their virtue, their spiritual consolations, and their hope of heaven. Nothing could be more untrue. The fact is that Nietzsche had no interest whatever in the delusions of the plain people—that is, intrinsically. It seemed to him of small moment *what* they believed, so long as it was safely imbecile. What he stood against was not their beliefs, but the elevation of those beliefs, by any sort of democratic process, to the dignity of a state philosophy—what he feared most was the pollution and crippling of the superior minority by intellectual disease from below. His plain aim in "The Antichrist" was to combat that menace by completing the work begun, on the one hand, by Darwin and the other evolutionist philosophers, and, on the other hand, by German historians and philologians. The net effect of this earlier attack, in the eighties, had been the collapse of Christian theology as a serious concern of educated men. The mob, it must be obvious, was very little shaken; even to this day it has not put off its belief in the essential Christian doctrines. But the *intelligentsia*, by 1885, had been pretty well convinced. No man of sound information, at the time Nietzsche planned "The Antichrist," actually believed that the world was created in seven days, or that its fauna was once overwhelmed by a flood as a penalty for the sins of man, or that Noah saved the boa constrictor, the prairie dog and the *pediculus capitis* by taking a pair of each into the ark, or that Lot's wife was turned into a pillar of salt, or that a fragment of the True Cross could cure hydrophobia.

Such notions, still almost universally prevalent in Christendom a century before, were now confined to the great body of ignorant and credulous men—that is, to ninety-five or ninety-six percent of the race. For a man of the superior minority to subscribe to one of them publicly was already sufficient to set him off as one in imminent need of psychiatrical attention. Belief in them had become a mark of inferiority, like the allied belief in madstones, magic and apparitions.

But though the theology of Christianity had thus sunk to the lowly estate of a mere delusion of the rabble, propagated on that level by the ancient caste of sacerdotal parasites, the ethics of Christianity continued to enjoy the utmost acceptance, and perhaps even more acceptance than ever before. It seemed to be generally felt, in fact, that they simply *must* be saved from the wreck—that the world would vanish into chaos if they went the way of the revelations supporting them. In this fear a great many judicious men joined, and so there arose what was, in essence, an absolutely new Christian cult—a cult, to wit, purged of all the supernaturalism superimposed upon the older cult by generations of theologians, and harking back to what was conceived to be the pure ethical doctrine of Jesus. This cult still flourishes; Protestantism tends to become identical with it; it invades Catholicism as Modernism; it is supported by great numbers of men whose intelligence is manifest and whose sincerity is not open to question. Even Nietzsche himself yielded to it in weak moments, as you will discover on examining his somewhat laborious effort to make Paul the villain of Christian theology, and Jesus no more than an innocent bystander. But this sentimental yielding never went far enough to distract his attention for long from his main idea, which was this: that Christian ethics were quite as dubious, at bottom, as Christian theology—that they were founded, just as surely as such childish fables as the story of Jonah and the whale, upon the peculiar prejudices and credulities, the special desires and appetites, of inferior men—that they warred upon the best interests of men of a better sort quite as unmistakably as the most extravagant of objective superstitions. In brief, what he saw in Christian ethics, under all the poetry and all the fine show of altruism and all the theoretical benefits therein, was a democratic effort to curb the egoism of the strong—a conspiracy of the *chandala* against the free functioning of their superiors, nay, against the free progress of mankind. This theory is the thing he exposes in "The Antichrist," bringing to the business his amazingly chromatic and exigent eloquence at its finest flower. This is the "conspiracy" he sets forth in all the panoply of his characteristic italics, dashes, *sforzando* interjections and exclamation points.

Well, an idea is an idea. The present one may be right and it may be wrong. One thing is quite certain: that no progress will be made against it by denouncing it as merely immoral. If it is ever laid at all, it must be laid evidentially, logically. The notion to the contrary is thoroughly democratic; the mob is the most ruthless of tyrants; it is always in a democratic society that heresy and felony tend to be most constantly confused. One hears without surprise of a Bismarck philosophizing placidly (at least in his old age) upon the delusion of Socialism and of a Frederick the Great playing the hose of his cynicism upon the absolutism that was almost identical with his own person, but men in the mass never brook the destructive discussion of their fundamental beliefs, and that impatience is naturally most evident in those societies in which men in the mass are most influential. Democracy and free speech are not facets of one gem; democracy and free speech are eternal enemies. But in any battle between an institution and an idea, the idea, in the long run, has the better of it.

Here I do not venture into the absurdity of arguing that, as the world wags on, the truth always survives. I believe nothing of the sort. As a matter of fact, it seems to me that an idea that happens to be true—or, more exactly, as near to truth as any human idea can be, and yet remain generally intelligible—it seems to me that such an idea carries a special and often fatal handicap. The majority of men prefer delusion to truth. It soothes. It is easy to grasp. Above all, it fits more snugly than the truth into a universe of false appearances—of complex and irrational phenomena, defectively grasped. But though an idea that is true is thus not likely to prevail, an idea that is *attacked* enjoys a great advantage. The evidence behind it is now supported by sympathy, the sporting instinct, sentimentality—and sentimentality is as powerful as an army with banners. One never hears of a martyr in history whose notions are seriously disputed today. The forgotten ideas are those of the men who put them forward soberly and quietly, hoping fatuously that they would conquer by the force of their truth; these are the ideas that we now struggle to rediscover. Had Nietzsche lived to be burned at the stake by outraged Mississippi Methodists, it would have been a glorious day for his doctrines. As it is, they are helped on their way every time they are denounced as immoral and against God. The war brought down upon them the maledictions of vast herds of right-thinking men. And now "The Antichrist," after fifteen years of neglect, is being reprinted...

One imagines the author, a sardonic wraith, snickering somewhat sadly over the fact. His shade, wherever it suffers, is favoured in these days by many such consolations, some of them of much greater horsepower. Think of the facts and arguments, even the underlying theories and attitudes, that have been borrowed from him, consciously and unconsciously, by the foes of Bolshevism during these last thrilling years! The face of democracy, suddenly seen hideously close, has scared the guardians of the reigning plutocracy half to death, and they have gone to the devil himself for aid. Southern Senators, almost illiterate men, have mixed his acids with well water and spouted them like affrighted geysers, not knowing what they did. Nor are they the first to borrow from him. Years ago I called attention to the debt incurred with characteristic forgetfulness of obligation by the late Theodore Roosevelt, in "The Strenuous Life" and elsewhere. Roosevelt, a typical apologist for the existing order, adeptly dragging a herring across the trail whenever it was menaced, yet managed to delude the native boobery, at least until toward the end, into accepting him as a fiery exponent of pure democracy. Perhaps he even fooled himself; charlatans usually do so soon or late. A study of Nietzsche reveals the sources of much that was honest in him, and exposes the hollowness of much that was sham. Nietzsche, an infinitely harder and more courageous intellect, was incapable of any such confusion of ideas; he seldom allowed sentimentality to turn him from the glaring fact. What is called Bolshevism today he saw clearly a generation ago and described for what it was and is—democracy in another aspect, the old *ressentiment* of the lower orders in free function once more. Socialism, Puritanism, Philistinism, Christianity—he saw them all as allotropic forms of democracy, as variations upon the endless struggle of quantity against quality, of the weak and timorous against the strong and enterprising, of the botched against the fit. The world needed a staggering exaggeration to make it seem even half of the truth. It trembles today as it trembled during the French Revolution. Perhaps it would tremble less if it could combat the monster with a clearer conscience and less burden of compromising theory—if it could launch its forces frankly at the fundamental doctrine, and not merely employ them to police the transient orgy.

Nietzsche, in the long run, may help it toward that greater honesty. His notions, propagated by cuttings from cuttings from cuttings, may conceivably prepare the way for a sounder, more healthful theory of society and of the state, and so free human progress from the stupidities which now hamper it, and men of true vision from the despairs which now sicken them. I say it is conceivable, but I doubt that it is probable. The soul and the belly of mankind are too evenly balanced; it is not likely that the belly will ever put away its hunger or forget its power. Here, perhaps, there is an example of the eternal recurrence that Nietzsche was fond of mulling over in his blacker moods. We are in the midst of one of the perennial risings of the lower orders. It got under way long before any of the current Bolshevist demons was born; it was given its long, secure start by the intolerable tyranny of the plutocracy—the end product of the Eighteenth Century revolt against the old aristocracy. It found resistance suddenly slackened by civil war within the plutocracy itself—one gang of traders falling upon another gang, to the tune of vast hymn-singing and yells to God. Perhaps it has already passed its apogee; the plutocracy, chastened, shows signs of a new solidarity; the wheel continues to swing 'round. But this combat between proletariat and plutocracy is, after all, itself a civil war. Two inferiorities struggle for the privilege of polluting the world. What actual difference does it make to a civilized man, when there is a steel strike, whether the workmen win or the mill-owners win? The conflict can interest him only as spectacle, as the conflict between Bonaparte and the old order in Europe interested Goethe and Beethoven. The victory, whichever way it goes, will simply bring chaos nearer, and so set the stage for a genuine revolution later on, with (let us hope) a new feudalism or something better coming out of it, and a new Thirteenth Century at dawn. This seems to be the slow, costly way of the worst of habitable worlds.

In the present case my money is laid upon the plutocracy. It will win because it will be able, in the long run, to enlist the finer intelligences. The mob and its maudlin causes attract only sentimentalists and scoundrels, chiefly the latter. Politics, under a democracy, reduces itself to a mere struggle for office by flatterers of the proletariat; even when a superior man prevails at that disgusting game he must prevail at the cost of his self-respect. Not many superior men make the attempt. The average great captain of the rabble, when he is not simply a weeper over irremediable wrongs, is a hypocrite so far gone that he is unconscious of his own hypocrisy—a slimy fellow, offensive to the nose. The plutocracy can recruit measurably more respectable janissaries, if only because it can make self-interest less obviously costly to *amour propre.* Its defect and its weakness lie in the fact that it is still too young to have acquired dignity. But lately sprung from the mob it now preys upon, it yet shows some of the habits of mind of that mob: it is blatant, stupid, ignorant, lacking in all delicate instinct and governmental finesse. Above all, it remains somewhat heavily moral. One seldom finds it undertaking one of its characteristic imbecilities without offering a sonorous moral reason; it spends almost as much to support the Y. M. C. A., vice-crusading, Prohibition and other such puerilities as it spends upon Congressmen, strike-breakers, gun-men, kept patriots and newspapers. In Eng land the case is even worse. It is almost impossible to find a wealthy industrial over there who is not also an eminent non-conformist layman, and even among financiers there are praying brothers. On the Continent, the day is saved by the fact that the plutocracy tends to become more and more Jewish. Here the intellectual cynicism of the Jew almost counterbalances his social unpleasantness. If he is destined to lead the plutocracy of the world out of Little Bethel he will fail, of course, to turn it into an aristocracy—*i. e.*, a caste of gentlemen—, but he will at least make it clever, and hence worthy of consideration. The case against the Jews is long and damning; it would justify ten thousand times as many pogroms as now go on in the world. But whenever you find a Davidsbündlerschaft making practise against the Philistines, there you will find a Jew laying on. Maybe it was this fact that caused Nietzsche to speak up for the children of Israel quite as often as he spoke against them. He was not blind to their faults, but when he set them beside Christians he could not deny their general superiority. Perhaps in America and England, as on the Continent, the increasing Jewishness of the plutocracy, while cutting it off from all chance of ever developing into an aristocracy, will yet lift it to such a dignity that it will at least deserve a certain grudging respect.

But even so, it will remain in a sort of half-world, midway between the gutter and the stars. Above it will still stand the small group of men that constitutes the permanent aristocracy of the race—the men of imagination and high purpose, the makers of genuine progress, the brave and ardent spirits, above all petty fears and discontents and above all petty hopes and ideals no less. There were heroes before Agamemnon; there will be Bachs after Johann Sebastian. And beneath the Judaized plutocracy, the sublimated *bourgeoisie*, there the immemorial proletariat, I venture to guess, will roar on, endlessly tortured by its vain hatreds and envies, stampeded and made to tremble by its ancient superstitions, prodded and made miserable by its sordid and degrading hopes. It seems to me very likely that, in this proletariat, Christianity will continue to survive. It is nonsense, true enough, but it is sweet. Nietzsche, denouncing its dangers as a poison, almost falls into the error of denying it its undoubtedly sugary smack. Of all the religions ever devised by the great practical jokers of the race, this is the one that offers most for the least money, so to speak, to the inferior man. It starts out by denying his inferiority in plain terms: *all* men are equal in the sight of God. It ends by erecting that inferiority into a sort of actual superiority: it is a merit to be stupid, and miserable, and sorely put upon—of such are the celestial elect. Not all the eloquence of a million Nietzsches, nor all the painful marshalling of evidence of a million Darwins and Harnacks, will ever empty that great consolation of its allure. The most they can ever accomplish is to make the superior orders of men acutely conscious of the exact nature of it, and so give them armament against the contagion. This is going on; this is being done. I think that "The Antichrist" has a useful place in that enterprise. It is strident, it is often extravagant, it is, to many sensitive men, in the worst of possible taste, but at bottom it is enormously apt and effective—and on the surface it is undoubtedly a good show. One somehow enjoys, with the malice that is native to man, the spectacle of anathemas batted back; it is refreshing to see the pitchfork employed against gentlemen who have doomed such innumerable caravans to hell. In Nietzsche they found, after many long years, a foeman worthy of them—not a mere fancy swordsman like Voltaire, or a mob orator like Tom Paine, or a pedant like the heretics of exegesis, but a gladiator armed with steel and armoured with steel, and showing all the ferocious gusto of a mediaeval bishop. It is a pity that Holy Church has no process for the elevation of demons, like its process for the canonization of saints. There must be a long roll of black miracles to the discredit of the Accursed Friedrich—sinners purged of conscience and made happy in their sinning, clerics shaken in their theology by visions of a new and better holy city, the strong made to exult, the weak robbed of their old sad romance. It would be a pleasure to see the *Advocatus Diaboli* turn from the table of the prosecution to the table of the defence, and move in solemn form for the damnation of the Naumburg hobgoblin...

Of all Nietzsche's books, "The Antichrist" comes nearest to conventionality in form. It presents a connected argument with very few interludes, and has a beginning, a middle and an end. Most of his works are in the form of collections of apothegms, and sometimes the subject changes on every second page. This fact constitutes one of the counts in the orthodox indictment of him: it is cited as proof that his capacity for consecutive thought was limited, and that he was thus deficient mentally, and perhaps a downright moron. The argument, it must be obvious, is fundamentally nonsensical. What deceives the professors is the traditional prolixity of philosophers. Because the average philosophical writer, when he essays to expose his ideas, makes such inordinate drafts upon the parts of speech that the dictionary is almost emptied these defective observers jump to the conclusion that his intrinsic notions are of corresponding weight. This is not unseldom quite untrue. What makes philosophy so garrulous is not the profundity of philosophers, but their lack of art; they are like physicians who sought to cure a slight hyperacidity by giving the patient a carload of burned oyster-shells to eat. There is, too, the endless poll-parrotting that goes on: each new philosopher must prove his learning by laboriously rehearsing the ideas of all previous philosophers... Nietzsche avoided both faults. He always assumed that his readers knew the books, and that it was thus unnecessary to rewrite them. And, having an idea that seemed to him to be novel and original, he stated it in as few words as possible, and then shut down. Sometimes he got it into a hundred words; sometimes it took a thousand; now and then, as in the present case, he developed a series of related ideas into a connected book. But he never wrote a word too many. He never pumped up an idea to make it appear bigger than it actually was. The pedagogues, alas, are not accustomed to that sort of writing in serious fields. They resent it, and sometimes they even try to improve it. There exists, in fact, a huge and solemn tome on Nietzsche by a learned man of America in which all of his brilliancy is painfully translated into the windy phrases of the seminaries. The tome is satisfactorily ponderous, but the meat of the cocoanut is left out: there is actually no discussion of the Nietzschean view of Christianity!... Always Nietzsche daunts the pedants. He employed too few words for them—and he had too many ideas.

* * *

The present translation of "The Antichrist" is published by agreement with Dr. Oscar Levy, editor of the English edition of Nietzsche. There are two earlier translations, one by Thomas Common and the other by Anthony M. Ludovici. That of Mr. Common follows the text very closely, and thus occasionally shows some essentially German turns of phrase; that of Mr. Ludovici is more fluent but rather less exact. I do not offer my own version on the plea that either of these is useless; on the contrary, I cheerfully acknowledge that they have much merit, and that they helped me at almost every line. I began this new Englishing of the book, not in any hope of supplanting them, and surely not with any notion of meeting a great public need, but simply as a private amusement in troubled days. But as I got on with it I began to see ways of putting some flavour of Nietzsche's peculiar style into the English, and so amusement turned into a more or less serious labour. The result, of course, is far from satisfactory, but it at least represents a very diligent attempt. Nietzsche, always under the influence of French models, wrote a German that differs materially from any other German that I know. It is more nervous, more varied, more rapid in tempo; it runs to more effective climaxes; it is never stodgy. His marks begin to show upon the writing of the younger Germans of today. They are getting away from the old thunderous manner, with its long sentences and its tedious grammatical complexities. In the course of time, I daresay, they will develop a German almost as clear as French and almost as colourful and resilient as English.

I owe thanks to Dr. Levy for his *imprimatur*, to Mr. Theodor Hemberger for criticism, and to Messrs. Common and Ludovici for showing me the way around many a difficulty.

–H.L. Mencken

Preface

This book belongs to the most rare of men. Perhaps not one of them is yet alive. It is possible that they may be among those who understand my "Zarathustra": how *could* I confound myself with those who are now sprouting ears?—First the day after tomorrow must come for me. Some men are born posthumously.

The conditions under which any one understands me, and *necessarily* understands me—I know them only too well. Even to endure my seriousness, my passion, he must carry intellectual integrity to the verge of hardness. He must be accustomed to living on mountain tops—and to looking upon the wretched gabble of politics and nationalism as *beneath* him. He must have become indifferent; he must never ask of the truth whether it brings profit to him or a fatality to him... He must have an inclination, born of strength, for questions that no one has the courage for; the courage for the *forbidden*; predestination for the labyrinth. The experience of seven solitudes. New ears for new music. New eyes for what is most distant. A new conscience for truths that have hitherto remained unheard. *And* the will to economize in the grand manner—to hold together his strength, his enthusiasm... Reverence for self; love of self; absolute freedom of self...

Very well, then! of that sort only are my readers, my true readers, my readers foreordained: of what account are the *rest*?—The rest are merely humanity.—One must make one's self superior to humanity, in power, in *loftiness* of soul,—in contempt.

–Friedrich W. Nietzsche

The Antichrist

1

—Let us look each other in the face. We are Hyperboreans—we know well enough how remote our place is. "Neither by land nor by water will you find the road to the Hyperboreans": even Pindar,[1] in his day, knew *that* much about us. Beyond the North, beyond the ice, beyond *death—our* life, *our* happiness... We have discovered that happiness; we know the way; we got our knowledge of it from thousands of years in the labyrinth. Who *else* has found it?—The man of today?—"I don't know either the way out or the way in; I am whatever doesn't know either the way out or the way in"—so sighs the man of today... *This* is the sort of modernity that made us ill,—we sickened on lazy peace, cowardly compromise, the whole virtuous dirtiness of the modern Yea and Nay. This tolerance and *largeur* of the heart that "forgives"

1. *Cf.* the tenth Pythian ode. See also the fourth book of Herodotus. The Hyperboreans were a mythical people beyond the Rhipaean mountains, in the far North. They enjoyed unbroken happiness and perpetual youth.

everything because it "understands" everything is a sirocco to us. Rather live amid the ice than among modern virtues and other such south-winds!... We were brave enough; we spared neither ourselves nor others; but we were a long time finding out *where* to direct our courage. We grew dismal; they called us fatalists. *Our* fate—it was the fullness, the tension, the *storing up* of powers. We thirsted for the lightning's and great deeds; we kept as far as possible from the happiness of the weakling, from "resignation"... There was thunder in our air; nature, as we embodied it, became overcast—*for we had not yet found the way.* The formula of our happiness: a Yea, a Nay, a straight line, a *goal...*

2

What is good?—Whatever augments the feeling of power, the will to power, power itself, in man.

What is evil?—Whatever springs from weakness.

What is happiness?—The feeling that power *increases*—that resistance is overcome.

Not contentment, but more power; *not* peace at any price, but war; *not* virtue, but efficiency (virtue in the Renaissance sense, *virtu*, virtue free of moral acid).

The weak and the botched shall perish: first principle of *our* charity. And one should help them to it.

What is more harmful than any vice?—Practical sympathy for the botched and the weak—Christianity...

3

The problem that I set here is not what shall replace mankind in the order of living creatures (—man is an end—): but what type of man must be *bred*, must be *willed*, as being the most valuable, the most worthy of life, the most secure guarantee of the future.

This more valuable type has appeared often enough in the past: but always as a happy accident, as an exception, never as deliberately *willed*. Very often it has been precisely the most feared; hitherto it has been almost *the* terror of terrors;—and out of that terror the contrary type has been willed, cultivated and *attained*: the domestic animal, the herd animal, the sick brute-man—the Christian...

4

Mankind surely does *not* represent an evolution toward a better or stronger or higher level, as progress is now understood. This "progress" is merely a modern idea, which is to say, a false idea. The European of today, in his essential worth, falls far below the European of the Renaissance; the process of evolution does *not* necessarily mean elevation, enhancement, strengthening.

True enough, it succeeds in isolated and individual cases in various parts of the earth and under the most widely different cultures, and in these cases a *higher* type certainly manifests itself; something which, compared to mankind in the mass, appears as a sort of superman. Such happy strokes of high success have always been possible, and will remain possible, perhaps, for all time to come. Even whole races, tribes and nations may occasionally represent such lucky accidents.

5

We should not deck out and embellish Christianity: it has waged a war to the death against this *higher* type of man, it has put all the deepest instincts of this type under its ban, it has developed its concept of evil, of the Evil One himself, out of these instincts—the strong man as the typical reprobate, the "outcast among men." Christianity has taken the part of all the weak, the low, the botched; it has made an ideal out of *antagonism* to all the self-preservative instincts of sound life; it has corrupted even the faculties of those natures that are intellectually most vigorous, by representing the highest intellectual values as sinful, as misleading, as full of temptation. The most lamentable example: the corruption of Pascal, who believed that his intellect had been destroyed by original sin, whereas it was actually destroyed by Christianity!—

6

It is a painful and tragic spectacle that rises before me: I have drawn back the curtain from the *rottenness* of man. This word, in my mouth, is at least free from one suspicion: that it involves a moral accusation against humanity. It is used—and I wish to emphasize the fact again—without any moral significance: and this is so far true that the rottenness I speak of is most apparent to me precisely in those quarters where there has been most aspiration, hitherto, toward "virtue" and "godliness." As you probably surmise, I understand rottenness in the sense of *décadence*: my argument is that all the values on which mankind now fixes its highest aspirations are *décadence*-values.

I call an animal, a species, an individual corrupt, when it loses its instincts, when it chooses, when it *prefers*, what is injurious to it. A history of the "higher feelings," the "ideals of humanity"—and it is possible that I'll have to write it—would almost explain why man is so degenerate. Life itself appears to me as an instinct for growth, for survival, for the accumulation of forces, for *power*: whenever the will to power fails there is disaster. My contention is that all the highest values of humanity have been emptied of this will—that the values of *décadence*, of *nihilism*, now prevail under the holiest names.

7

Christianity is called the religion of *pity*.—Pity stands in opposition to all the tonic passions that augment the energy of the feeling of aliveness: it is a depressant. A man loses power when he pities. Through pity that drain upon strength which suffering works is multiplied a thousand fold. Suffering is made contagious by pity; under certain circumstances it may lead to a total sacrifice of life and living energy—a loss out of all proportion to the magnitude of the cause (—the case of the death of the Nazarene). This is the first view of it; there is, however, a still more important one. If one measures the effects of pity by the gravity of the reactions it sets up, its character as a menace to life appears in a much clearer light. Pity thwarts the whole law of evolution, which is the law of natural selection. It preserves whatever is ripe for destruction; it fights on the side of those disinherited and condemned by life; by maintaining life in so many of the botched of all kinds, it gives life itself a gloomy and dubious aspect. Mankind has ventured to call pity a virtue (—in every *superior* moral system it appears as a weakness—); going still further, it has been called *the* virtue, the source and foundation of all other virtues—but let us always bear in mind that this was from the standpoint of a philosophy that was nihilistic, and upon whose shield *the denial of life* was inscribed. Schopenhauer was right in this: that by means of pity life is denied, and made *worthy of denial*—pity is the technic of nihilism. Let me repeat: this depressing and contagious instinct stands against all those instincts which work for the preservation and enhancement of life: in the rôle of *protector* of the miserable, it is a prime agent in the promotion of *décadence*—pity persuades to extinction... Of course, one doesn't say "extinction": one says "the other world," or "God," or "the *true* life," or Nirvana, salvation, blessedness... This innocent rhetoric, from the realm of religious-ethical balderdash, appears *a good deal less innocent* when one reflects upon the tendency that it conceals beneath sublime words: the tendency to *destroy life*. Schopenhauer was hostile to life: that is why pity appeared to him as a virtue... Aristotle, as everyone knows, saw in pity a sickly and dangerous state of mind, the remedy for which was an occasional purgative: he regarded tragedy as that purgative. The instinct of life should prompt us to seek some means of puncturing any such pathological and dangerous accumulation of pity as that appearing in Schopenhauer's case (and also, alack, in that of our whole literary *décadence*, from St. Petersburg to Paris, from Tolstoi to Wagner), that it may burst and be discharged... Nothing is more unhealthy, amid all our unhealthy modernism, than Christian pity. To be the doctors *here*, to be unmerciful *here*, to wield the knife *here*—all this is *our* business, all this is *our* sort of humanity, by this sign we are philosophers, we Hyperboreans!—

8

It is necessary to say just *whom* we regard as our antagonists: theologians and all who have any theological blood in their veins—this is our whole philosophy... One must have faced that menace at close hand, better still, one must have had experience of it directly and almost succumbed to it, to realize that it is not to be taken lightly (—the alleged free-thinking of our naturalists and physiologists seems to me to be a joke—they have no passion about such things; they have not suffered—). This poisoning goes a great deal further than most people think: I find the arrogant habit of the theologian among all who regard themselves as "idealists"—among all who, by virtue of a higher point of departure, claim a right to rise above reality, and to look upon it with suspicion... The idealist, like the ecclesiastic, carries all sorts of lofty concepts in his hand (—and not only in his hand!); he launches them with benevolent contempt against "understanding," "the senses," "honor," "good living," "science"; he sees such things as *beneath* him, as pernicious and seductive forces, on which "the soul" soars as a pure thing-in-itself—as if humility, chastity, poverty, in a word, *holiness*, had not already done much more damage to life than all imaginable horrors and vices... The pure soul is a pure lie... So long as the priest, that *professional* denier, calumniator and poisoner of life, is accepted as a *higher* variety of man, there can be no answer to the question, What *is* truth? Truth has already been stood on its head when the obvious attorney of mere emptiness is mistaken for its representative...

9

Upon this theological instinct I make war: I find the tracks of it everywhere. Whoever has theological blood in his veins is shifty and dishonourable in all things. The pathetic thing that grows out of this condition is called *faith*: in other words, closing one's eyes upon one's self once for all, to avoid suffering the sight of incurable falsehood. People erect a concept of morality, of virtue, of holiness upon this false view of all things; they ground good conscience upon faulty vision; they argue that no *other* sort of vision has value any more, once they have made their sacrosanct with the names of "God," "salvation" and "eternity." I unearth this theological instinct in all directions: it is the most widespread and the most *subterranean* form of falsehood to be found on earth. Whatever a theologian regards as true *must* be false: there you have almost a criterion of truth. His profound instinct of self-preservation stands against truth ever coming into honour in any way, or even getting stated. Wherever the in fluence of theologians is felt there is a transvaluation of values, and the concepts "true" and "false" are forced to change places: whatever is most damaging to life is there called "true," and whatever exalts it, intensifies it, approves it, justifies it and makes it triumphant is there called "false."... When theologians, working through the "consciences" of princes (or of peoples—), stretch out their hands for *power*, there is never any doubt as to the fundamental issue: the will to make an end, the *nihilistic* will exerts that power...

10

Among Germans I am immediately understood when I say that theological blood is the ruin of philosophy. The Protestant pastor is the grandfather of German philosophy; Protestantism itself is its *peccatum originale.* Definition of Protestantism: hemiplegic paralysis of Christianity—*and* of reason... One need only utter the words "Tübingen School" to get an understanding of what German philosophy is at bottom—a very artful form of theology... The Suabians are the best liars in Germany; they lie innocently... Why all the rejoicing over the appearance of Kant that went through the learned world of Germany, three-fourths of which is made up of the sons of preachers and teachers—why the German conviction still echoing, that with Kant came a change for the *better*? The theological instinct of German scholars made them see clearly just *what* had become possible again... A backstairs leading to the old ideal stood open; the concept of the "true world," the concept of morality as the *essence* of the world (—the two most vicious errors that ever existed!), were once more, thanks to a subtle and wily scepticism, if not actually demonstrable, then *at least* no longer *refutable... Reason*, the *prerogative* of reason, does not go so far... Out of reality there had been made "appearance"; an absolutely false world, that of being, had been turned into reality... The success of Kant is merely a theological success; he was, like Luther and Leibnitz, but one more impediment to German integrity, already far from steady.—

11

A word now against Kant as a moralist. A virtue must be *our* invention; it must spring out of *our* personal need and defence. In every other case it is a source of danger. That which does not belong to our life *menaces* it; a virtue which has its roots in mere respect for the concept of "virtue," as Kant would have it, is pernicious. "Virtue," "duty," "good for its own sake," goodness grounded upon impersonality or a notion of universal validity—these are all chimeras, and in them one finds only an expression of the decay, the last collapse of life, the Chinese spirit of Königsberg. Quite the contrary is demanded by the most profound laws of self-preservation and of growth: to wit, that every man find his *own* virtue, his *own* categorical imperative. A nation goes to pieces when it confounds *its* duty with the general concept of duty. Nothing works a more complete and penetrating disaster than every "impersonal" duty, every sacrifice before the Moloch of abstraction.—To think that no one has thought of Kant's categorical imperative as *dangerous to life*!... The theological instinct alone took it under protection!—An action prompted by the life-instinct proves that it is a *right* action by the amount of pleasure that goes with it: and yet that Nihilist, with his bowels of Christian dogmatism, regarded pleasure as an *objection*... What destroys a man more quickly than to work, think and feel without inner necessity, without any deep personal desire, without pleasure—as a mere automaton of duty? That is the recipe for *décadence*, and no less for idiocy... Kant became an idiot.—And such a man was the contemporary of Goethe! This calamitous spinner of cobwebs passed for *the* German philosopher—still passes today!... I forbid myself to say what I think of the Germans...

Didn't Kant see in the French Revolution the transformation of the state from the inorganic form to the *organic*? Didn't he ask himself if there was a single event that could be explained save on the assumption of a moral faculty in man, so that on the basis of it, "the tendency of mankind toward the good" could be *explained*, once and for all time? Kant's answer: "That is revolution." Instinct at fault in everything and anything, instinct as a revolt against nature, German *décadence* as a philosophy—*that is Kant!*—

12

I put aside a few sceptics, the types of decency in the history of philosophy: the rest haven't the slightest conception of intellectual integrity. They behave like women, all these great enthusiasts and prodigies—they regard "beautiful feelings" as arguments, the "heaving breast" as the bellows of divine inspiration, conviction as the *criterion* of truth. In the end, with "German" innocence, Kant tried to give a scientific flavour to this form of corruption, this dearth of intellectual conscience, by calling it "practical reason." He deliberately invented a variety of reasons for use on occasions when it was desirable not to trouble with reason—that is, when morality, when the sublime command "thou shalt," was heard. When one recalls the fact that, among all peoples, the philosopher is no more than a development from the old type of priest, this inheritance from the priest, this *fraud upon self*, ceases to be remarkable. When a man feels that he has a divine mission, say to lift up, to save or to liberate mankind—when a man feels the divine spark in his heart and believes that he is the mouthpiece of super natural imperatives—when such a mission inflames him, it is only natural that he should stand beyond all merely reasonable standards of judgment. He feels that he is *himself* sanctified by this mission, that he is himself a type of a higher order!... What has a priest to do with philosophy! He stands far above it!—And hitherto the priest has *ruled*!—He has determined the meaning of "true" and "not true"!...

13

Let us not underestimate this fact: that *we ourselves*, we free spirits, are already a "transvaluation of all values," a *visualized* declaration of war and victory against all the old concepts of "true" and "not true." The most valuable intuitions are the last to be attained; the most valuable of all are those which determine *methods*. All the methods, all the principles of the scientific spirit of today, were the targets for thousands of years of the most profound contempt; if a man inclined to them he was excluded from the society of "decent" people—he passed as "an enemy of God," as a scoffer at the truth, as one "possessed." As a man of science, he belonged to the Chandala[1]... We have had the whole pathetic stupidity of mankind against us—their every notion of what the truth *ought* to be, of what the service of the truth *ought* to be—their every "thou shalt" was launched against us... Our objectives, our methods, our quiet, cautious, distrustful manner—all appeared to them as absolutely discreditable and contemptible.—Looking back, one may almost ask one's self with reason if it was not actually an *aesthetic* sense that kept men blind so long: what they demanded of the truth was picturesque effectiveness, and of the learned a strong appeal to their senses.

1. The lowest of the Hindu castes.

It was our *modesty* that stood out longest against their taste... How well they guessed that, these turkey-cocks of God!

14

We have unlearned something. We have become more modest in every way. We no longer derive man from the "spirit," from the "godhead"; we have dropped him back among the beasts. We regard him as the strongest of the beasts because he is the craftiest; one of the results thereof is his intellectuality. On the other hand, we guard ourselves against a conceit which would assert itself even here: that man is the great second thought in the process of organic evolution. He is, in truth, anything but the crown of creation: beside him stand many other animals, all at similar stages of development... And even when we say that we say a bit too much, for man, relatively speaking, is the most botched of all the animals and the sickliest, and he has wandered the most dangerously from his instincts—though for all that, to be sure, he remains the most *interesting*!—As regards the lower animals, it was Descartes who first had the really admirable daring to describe them as *machina*; the whole of our physiology is directed toward proving the truth of this doctrine. Moreover, it is illogical to set man apart, as Descartes did: what we know of man today is limited precisely by the extent to which we have regarded him, too, as a machine. Formerly we accorded to man, as his inheritance from some higher order of beings, what was called "free will"; now we have taken even this will from him, for the term no longer describes anything that we can understand. The old word "will" now connotes only a sort of result, an individual reaction, that follows inevitably upon a series of partly discordant and partly harmonious stimuli—the will no longer "acts," or "moves."... Formerly it was thought that man's consciousness, his "spirit," offered evidence of his high origin, his divinity. That he might be *perfected*, he was advised, tortoise-like, to draw his senses in, to have no traffic with earthly things, to shuffle off his mortal coil—then only the important part of him, the "pure spirit," would remain. Here again we have thought out the thing better: to us consciousness, or "the spirit," appears as a symptom of a relative imperfection of the organism, as an experiment, a groping, a misunderstanding, as an affliction which uses up nervous force unnecessarily—we deny that anything can be done perfectly so long as it is done consciously. The "pure spirit" is a piece of pure stupidity: take away the nervous system and the senses, the so-called "mortal shell," and *the rest is miscalculation*—that is all!...

15

Under Christianity neither morality nor religion has any point of contact with actuality. It offers purely imaginary *causes* ("God," "soul," "ego," "spirit," "free will"—or even "unfree"), and purely imaginary *effects* ("sin," "salvation," "grace," "punishment," "forgiveness of sins"). Intercourse between imaginary *beings* ("God," "spirits," "souls"); an imaginary *natural history* (anthropocentric; a total denial of the concept of natural causes); an imaginary *psychology* (misunderstandings of self, misinterpretations of agreeable or disagreeable general feelings—for example, of the states of the *nervus sympathicus* with the help of the sign-language of religio-ethical balderdash—, "repentance," "pangs of conscience," "temptation by the devil," "the presence of God");

an imaginary *teleology* (the "kingdom of God," "the last judgment," "eternal life").—This purely *fictitious world*, greatly to its disadvantage, is to be differentiated from the world of dreams; the latter at least reflects reality, whereas the former falsifies it, cheapens it and denies it. Once the concept of "nature" had been opposed to the concept of "God," the word "natural" necessarily took on the meaning of "abominable"—the whole of that fictitious world has its sources in hatred of the natural (—the real!—), and is no more than evidence of a profound uneasiness in the presence of reality... *This explains everything.* Who alone has any reason for living his way out of reality? The man who suffers under it. But to suffer from reality one must be a *botched* reality... The preponderance of pains over pleasures is the cause of this fictitious morality and religion: but such a preponderance also supplies the formula for *décadence*...

16

A criticism of the *Christian concept of God* leads inevitably to the same conclusion.—A nation that still believes in itself holds fast to its own god. In him it does honour to the conditions which enable it to survive, to its virtues—it projects its joy in itself, its feeling of power, into a being to whom one may offer thanks. He who is rich will give of his riches; a proud people need a god to whom they can make *sacrifices*... Religion, within these limits, is a form of gratitude. A man is grateful for his own existence: to that end he needs a god.—Such a god must be able to work both benefits and injuries; he must be able to play either friend or foe—he is wondered at for the good he does as well as for the evil he does. But the castration, against all nature, of such a god, making him a god of goodness alone, would be contrary to human inclination. Mankind has just as much need for an evil god as for a good god; it doesn't have to thank mere tolerance and humanitarianism for its own existence... What would be the value of a god who knew nothing of anger, revenge, envy, scorn, cunning, violence? who had perhaps never experienced the rapturous *ardeurs* of victory and of destruction? No one would understand such a god: why should anyone want him?—True enough, when a nation is on the downward path, when it feels its belief in its own future, its hope of freedom slipping from it, when it begins to see submission as a first necessity and the virtues of submission as measures of self-preservation, then it *must* overhaul its god. He then becomes a hypocrite, timorous and demure; he counsels "peace of soul," hate-no-more, leniency, "love" of friend and foe. He moralizes endlessly; he creeps into every private virtue; he becomes the god of every man; he becomes a private citizen, a cosmopolitan... Formerly he represented a people, the strength of a people, everything aggressive and thirsty for power in the soul of a people; now he is simply *the good god*... The truth is that there is no other alternative for gods: *either* they are the will to power—in which case they are national gods—*or* incapacity for power—in which case they have to be good...

17

Wherever the will to power begins to decline, in whatever form, there is always an accompanying decline physiologically, a *décadence*. The divinity of this *décadence*, shorn of its masculine virtues and passions, is converted perforce into a god of the physiologically degraded, of the weak. Of course, they do not *call* themselves the weak; they call themselves "the good."... No hint is needed to indicate the moments in history at which the dualistic fiction of a good and an evil god first became possible. The same instinct which prompts the inferior to reduce their own god to "goodness-in-itself" also prompts them to eliminate all good qualities from the god of their superiors; they make revenge on their masters by making a *devil* of the latter's god.—The *good* god, and the devil like him—both are abortions of *décadence*.—How can we be so tolerant of the naïveté of Christian theologians as to join in their doctrine that the evolution of the concept of god from "the god of Israel," the god of a people, to the Christian god, the essence of all goodness, is to be described as *progress*?—But even Renan does this. As if Renan had a right to be naïve! The contrary actually stares one in the face. When everything necessary to *ascending* life; when all that is strong, courageous, masterful and proud has been eliminated from the concept of a god; when he has sunk step by step to the level of a staff for the weary, a sheet-anchor for the drowning; when he becomes the poor man's god, the sinner's god, the invalid's god *par excellence*, and the attribute of "saviour" or "redeemer" remains as the one essential attribute of divinity—just *what* is the significance of such a metamorphosis? what does such a *reduction* of the godhead imply?—To be sure, the "kingdom of God" has thus grown larger. Formerly he had only his own people, his "chosen" people. But since then he has gone wandering, like his people themselves, into foreign parts; he has given up settling down quietly anywhere; finally he has come to feel at home everywhere, and is the great cosmopolitan—until now he has the "great majority" on his side, and half the earth. But this god of the "great majority," this democrat among gods, has not become a proud heathen god: on the contrary, he remains a Jew, he remains a god in a corner, a god of all the dark nooks and crevices, of all the noise some quarters of the world!... His earthly kingdom, now as always, is a kingdom of the underworld, a *souterrain* kingdom, a ghetto kingdom... And he himself is so pale, so weak, so *décadent*... Even the palest of the pale are able to master him—messieurs the metaphysicians, those albinos of the intellect. They spun their webs around him for so long that finally he was hypnotized, and began to spin himself, and became another metaphysician. Thereafter he resumed once more his old business of spinning the world out of his inmost being *sub specie Spinozae*; thereafter he became ever thinner and paler—became the "ideal," became "pure spirit," became "the absolute," became "the thing-in-itself."... *The collapse of a god*: he became a "thing-in-itself."

18

The Christian concept of a god—the god as the patron of the sick, the god as a spinner of cobwebs, the god as a spirit—is one of the most corrupt concepts that has ever been set up in the world: it probably touches low-water mark in the ebbing evolution of the god-type. God degenerated into the *contradiction of life*. Instead of being its transfiguration and eternal Yea! In him war is declared on life, on nature, on the will to live! God becomes the formula for every slander upon the "here and now," and for every lie about the "beyond"! In him nothingness is deified, and the will to nothingness is made holy!...

19

The fact that the strong races of northern Europe did not repudiate this Christian god does little credit to their gift for religion—and not much more to their taste. They ought to have been able to make an end of such a moribund and worn-out product of the *décadence*. A curse lies upon them because they were not equal to it; they made illness, decrepitude and contradiction a part of their instincts—and since then they have not managed to *create* any more gods. Two thousand years have come and gone—and not a single new god! Instead, there still exists, and as if by some intrinsic right,—as if he were the *ultimatum* and *maximum* of the power to create gods, of the *creator spiritus* in mankind—this pitiful god of Christian monotono-theism! This hybrid image of decay, conjured up out of emptiness, contradiction and vain imagining, in which all the instincts of *décadence*, all the cowardices and wearinesses of the soul find their sanction!—

20

In my condemnation of Christianity I surely hope I do no injustice to a related religion with an even larger number of believers: I allude to *Buddhism*. Both are to be reckoned among the nihilistic religions—they are both *décadence* religions—but they are separated from each other in a very remarkable way. For the fact that he is able to *compare* them at all the critic of Christianity is indebted to the scholars of India.—Buddhism is a hundred times as realistic as Christianity—it is part of its living heritage that it is able to face problems objectively and coolly; it is the product of long centuries of philosophical speculation. The concept, "god," was already disposed of before it appeared. Buddhism is the only genuinely *positive* religion to be encountered in history, and this applies even to its epistemology (which is a strict phenomenalism). It does not speak of a "struggle with sin," but, yielding to reality, of the "struggle with suffering." Sharply differentiating itself from Christianity, it puts the self-deception that lies in moral concepts behind it; it is, in my phrase, *beyond* good and evil.—The two physiological facts upon which it grounds itself and upon which it bestows its chief attention are: first, an excessive sensitiveness to sensation, which manifests itself as a refined susceptibility to pain, and *secondly*, an extraordinary spirituality, a too protracted concern with concepts and logical procedures, under the influence of which the instinct of personality has yielded to a notion of the "impersonal." (—Both of these states will be familiar to a few of my readers, the objectivists, by experience, as they are to me). These physiological states produced a *depression*, and Buddha tried to combat it by hygienic measures. Against it he prescribed a life in the open, a life of travel; moderation in eating and a careful selection of foods; caution in the use of intoxicants; the same caution in arousing any of the passions that foster a bilious habit and heat the blood; finally, no *worry*, either on one's own account or on account of others. He encourages ideas that make for either quiet contentment or good cheer—he finds means to combat ideas of other sorts. He understands good, the state of goodness, as something which promotes health. *Prayer* is not included, and neither is *asceticism*. There is no categorical imperative nor any disciplines, even within the walls of a monastery (—it is always possible to leave—). These things would have been simply means of increasing the excessive sensitiveness above mentioned. For the same reason he does not advocate any conflict with unbelievers; his teaching is antagonistic to nothing so much as to revenge, aversion, *ressentiment* (—"enmity never brings an end to enmity": the moving refrain of all Buddhism...) And in all this he was right, for it is precisely these passions which, in view of his main regiminal purpose, are *unhealthful.* The mental fatigue that he observes, already plainly displayed in too much "objectivity" (that is, in the individual's loss of interest in himself, in loss of balance and of "egoism"), he combats by strong efforts to lead even the spiritual interests back to the *ego.* In Buddha's teaching egoism is a duty. The "one thing needful," the question "how can you be delivered from suffering," regulates and determines the whole spiritual diet. (—Perhaps one will here recall that Athenian who also declared war upon pure "scientificality," to wit, Socrates, who also elevated egoism to the estate of a morality).

21

The things necessary to Buddhism are a very mild climate, customs of great gentleness and liberality, and *no* militarism; moreover, it must get its start among the higher and better educated classes. Cheerfulness, quiet and the absence of desire are the chief desiderata, and they are *attained.* Buddhism is not a religion in which perfection is merely an object of aspiration: perfection is actually normal.—

Under Christianity the instincts of the subjugated and the oppressed come to the fore: it is only those who are at the bottom who seek their salvation in it. Here the prevailing pastime, the favourite remedy for boredom is the discussion of sin, self-criticism, the inquisition of conscience; here the emotion produced by *power* (called "God") is pumped up (by prayer); here the highest good is regarded as unattainable, as a gift, as "grace." Here, too, open dealing is lacking; concealment and the darkened room are Christian. Her body is despised and hygiene is denounced as sensual; the church even ranges itself against cleanliness (—the first Christian order after the banishment of the Moors closed the public baths, of which there were 270 in Cordova alone). Christian, too, is a certain cruelty toward one's self and toward others; hatred of unbelievers; the will to persecute. Sombre and disquieting ideas are in the foreground; the most esteemed states of mind, bearing the most respectable names, are epileptoid; the diet is so regulated as to engender morbid symptoms and over-stimulate the nerves. Christian, again, is all deadly enmity to the rulers of the earth, to the "aristocratic"—along with a sort of secret rivalry with them (—one resigns one's "body" to them; one wants *only* one's "soul"...). And Christian is all hatred of the intellect, of pride, of courage, of freedom, of intellectual *libertinage*; Christian is all hatred of the senses, of joy in the senses, of joy in general...

22

When Christianity departed from its native soil, that of the lowest orders, the *underworld* of the ancient world, and began seeking power among barbarian peoples, it no longer had to deal with *exhausted* men, but with men still inwardly savage and capable of self-torture—in brief, strong men, but bungled men. Here, unlike in the case of the Buddhists, the cause of discontent with self, suffering through self, is *not* merely a general sensitiveness and susceptibility to pain, but, on the contrary, an inordinate thirst for inflicting pain on others, a tendency to obtain subjective satisfaction in hostile deeds and ideas. Christianity had to embrace *barbaric* concepts and valuations in order to obtain mastery over barbarians: of such sort, for example, are the sacrifices of the first-born, the drinking of blood as a sacrament, the disdain of the intellect and of culture; torture in all its forms, whether bodily or not; the whole pomp of the cult. Buddhism is a religion for peoples in a further state of development, for races that have become kind, gentle and over-spiritualized (—Europe is not yet ripe for it—): it is a summons that takes them back to peace and cheerfulness, to a careful rationing of the spirit, to a certain hardening of the body. Christianity aims at mastering *beasts of prey*; its modus operandi is to make them *ill*—to make feeble is the Christian recipe for taming, for "*civilizing.*" Buddhism is a religion for the closing, over-wearied stages of civilization. Christianity appears before civilization has so much as begun—under certain circumstances it lays the very foundations thereof.

23

Buddhism, I repeat, is a hundred times more austere, more honest, more objective. It no longer has to *justify* its pains, its susceptibility to suffering, by interpreting these things in terms of sin—it simply says, as it simply thinks, "I suffer." To the barbarian, however, suffering in itself is scarcely understandable: what he needs, first of all, is an explanation as to *why* he suffers. (His mere instinct prompts him to deny his suffering altogether, or to endure it in silence.) Here the word "devil" was a blessing: man had to have an omnipotent and terrible enemy—there was no need to be ashamed of suffering at the hands of such an enemy.—

At the bottom of Christianity there are several subtleties that belong to the Orient. In the first place, it knows that it is of very little consequence whether a thing be true or not, so long as it is *believed* to be true. Truth and *faith*: here we have two wholly distinct worlds of ideas, almost two diametrically *opposite* worlds—the road to the one and the road to the other lie miles apart. To understand that fact thoroughly—this is almost enough, in the Orient, to *make* one a sage. The Brahmins knew it, Plato knew it, every student of the esoteric knows it. When, for example, a man gets any *pleasure* out of the notion that he has been saved from sin, it is *not* necessary for him to be actually sinful, but merely to *feel* sinful. But when *faith* is thus exalted above everything else, it necessarily follows that reason, knowledge and patient inquiry have to be discredited: the road to the truth becomes a forbidden road.—Hope, in its stronger forms, is a great deal more powerful *stimulans* to life than any sort of realized joy can ever be. Man must be sustained in suffering by a hope so high that no conflict with actuality can dash it—so high, indeed, that no fulfilment can *satisfy* it: a hope reaching out beyond this world. (Precisely because of this power that hope has of making the suffering hold out, the Greeks regarded it as the evil of evils, as the most *malign* of evils; it remained behind at the source of all evil.)[1]—In order that *love* may be possible, God must become a person; in order that the lower instincts may take a hand in the matter God must be young. To satisfy the ardor of the woman a beautiful saint must appear on the scene, and to satisfy that of the men there must be a virgin. These things

1. That is, in Pandora's box.

are necessary if Christianity is to assume lordship over a soil on which some aphrodisiacal or Adonis cult has already established a notion as to what a cult ought to be. To insist upon *chastity* greatly strengthens the vehemence and subjectivity of the religious instinct—it makes the cult warmer, more enthusiastic, more soulful.—Love is the state in which man sees things most decidedly as they are *not*. The force of illusion reaches its highest here, and so does the capacity for sweetening, for *transfiguring*. When a man is in love he endures more than at any other time; he submits to anything. The problem was to devise a religion which would allow one to love: by this means the worst that life has to offer is overcome—it is scarcely even noticed.—So much for the three Christian virtues: faith, hope and charity: I call them the three Christian *ingenuities*.—Buddhism is in too late a stage of development, too full of positivism, to be shrewd in any such way.—

24

Here I barely touch upon the problem of the *origin* of Christianity. The *first* thing necessary to its solution is this: that Christianity is to be understood only by examining the soil from which it sprung—it is *not* a reaction against Jewish instincts; it is their inevitable product; it is simply one more step in the awe-inspiring logic of the Jews. In the words of the Saviour, "salvation is of the Jews."[1]—The *second* thing to remember is this: that the psychological type of the Galilean is still to be recognized, but it was only in its most degenerate form (which is at once maimed and overladen with foreign features) that it could serve

1. John iv, 22.

in the manner in which it has been used: as a type of the *Saviour* of mankind.—

The Jews are the most remarkable people in the history of the world, for when they were confronted with the question, to be or not to be, they chose, with perfectly unearthly deliberation, to be *at any price*: this price involved a radical *falsification* of all nature, of all naturalness, of all reality, of the whole inner world, as well as of the outer. They put themselves *against* all those conditions under which, hitherto, a people had been able to live, or had even been *permitted* to live; out of themselves they evolved an idea which stood in direct opposition to *natural* conditions—one-by-one they distorted religion, civilization, morality, history and psychology until each became a *contradiction* of its *natural significance*. We meet with the same phenomenon later on, in an incalculably exaggerated form, but only as a copy: the Christian church, put beside the "people of God," shows a complete lack of any claim to originality. Precisely for this reason the Jews are the most *fateful* people in the history of the world: their influence has so falsified the reasoning of mankind in this matter that today the Christian can cherish anti-Semitism without realizing that it is no more than the *final consequence of Judaism*.

In my "Genealogy of Morals" I give the first psychological explanation of the concepts underlying those two antithetical things, a *noble* morality and a *ressentiment* morality, the second of which is a mere product of the denial of the former. The Judaeo-Christian moral system belongs to the second division, and in every detail. In order to be able to say Nay to everything representing an *ascending* evolution of life—that is, to well-being, to power, to beauty, to self-approval—the instincts of *ressentiment*, here become downright genius, had to invent an *other*world in which the *acceptance of life* appeared as the most evil and abominable thing imaginable. Psychologically, the Jews are a people gifted with the very strongest vitality, so much so that when they found themselves facing impossible conditions of life they chose voluntarily, and with a profound talent for self-preservation, the side of all those instincts which make for *décadence—not* as if mastered by them, but as if detecting in them a power by which "the world" could be *defied*. The Jews are the very opposite of *décadents*: they have simply been forced into *appearing* in that guise, and with a degree of skill approaching the *non plus ultra* of histrionic genius they have managed to put themselves at the head of all *décadent* movements (—for example, the Christianity of Paul—), and so make of them something stronger than any party frankly saying *Yes* to life. To the sort of men who reach out for power under Judaism and Christianity,—that is to say, to the *priestly* class—*décadence* is no more than a means to an end. Men of this sort have a vital interest in making mankind sick, and in confusing the values of "good" and "bad," "true" and "false" in a manner that is not only dangerous to life, but also slanders it.

25

The history of Israel is invaluable as a typical history of an attempt to *denaturize* all natural values: I point to five facts which bear this out. Originally, and above all in the time of the monarchy, Israel maintained the *right* attitude of things, which is to say, the natural attitude. Its Jahveh was an expression of its consciousness of power, its joy in itself, its hopes for itself: to him the Jews looked for victory and salvation and through him they expected nature to give them whatever was necessary to their existence—above all, rain. Jahveh is the god of Israel, and *consequently* the god of justice: this is the logic of every race that has power in its hands and a good conscience in the use of it. In the religious ceremonial of the Jews both aspects of this self-approval stand revealed. The nation is grateful for the high destiny that has enabled it to obtain dominion; it is grateful for the benign procession of the seasons, and for the good fortune attending its herds and its crops.—This view of things remained an ideal for a long while, even after it had been robbed of validity by tragic blows: anarchy within and the Assyrian without. But the people still retained, as a projection of their highest yearnings, that vision of a king who was at once a gallant warrior and an upright judge—a vision best visualized in the typical prophet (*i. e.*, critic and satirist of the moment), Isaiah.—But every hope remained unfulfilled. The old god no longer *could* do what he used to do. He ought to have been abandoned. But what actually happened? Simply this: the conception of him was *changed*—the conception of him was *denaturized*; this was the price that had to be paid for keeping him.—Jahveh, the god of "justice"—he is in accord with Israel *no more*, he no longer vizualizes the national egoism; he is now a god only conditionally... The public notion of this god now becomes merely a weapon in the hands of clerical agitators, who interpret all happiness as a reward and all unhappiness as a punishment for obedience or disobedience to him, for "sin": that most fraudulent of all imaginable interpretations, whereby a "moral order of the world" is set up, and the fundamental concepts, "cause" and "effect," are stood on their heads. Once natural causation has been swept out of the world by doctrines of reward and punishment some sort of *un*-natural causation becomes necessary: and all other varieties of the denial of nature follow it. A god who *demands*—in place of a god who helps, who gives counsel, who is at bottom merely a name for every happy inspiration of courage and self-reliance... *Morality* is no longer a reflection of the conditions which make for the sound life and development of the people; it is no longer the primary life-instinct; instead it has become abstract and in opposition to life—a fundamental perversion of the fancy, an "evil eye" on all things. *What* is Jewish, *what* is Christian morality? Chance robbed of its innocence; unhappiness polluted with the idea of "sin"; well-being represented as a danger, as a "temptation"; a physiological disorder produced by the canker worm of conscience...

26

The concept of god falsified; the concept of morality falsified;—but even here Jewish priest-craft did not stop. The whole history of Israel ceased to be of any value: out with it!—These priests accomplished that miracle of falsification of which a great part of the Bible is the documentary evidence; with a degree of contempt unparalleled, and in the face of all tradition and all historical reality, they translated the past of their people into *religious* terms, which is to say, they converted it into an idiotic mechanism of salvation, whereby all offences against Jahveh were punished and all devotion to him was rewarded. We would regard this act of historical falsification as something far more shameful if familiarity with the *ecclesiastical* interpretation of history for thousands of years had not blunted our inclinations for uprightness *in historicis*. And the philosophers support the church: the *lie* about a "moral order of the world" runs through the whole of philosophy, even the newest. What is the meaning of a "moral order of the world"? That there is a thing called the will of God which, once and for all time, determines what man ought to do and what he ought not to do; that the worth of a people, or of an individual thereof, is to be measured by the extent to which they or he obey this will of God; that the destinies of a people or of an individual are *controlled* by this will of God, which rewards or punishes according to the degree of obedience manifested.—In place of all that pitiable lie *reality* has this to say: the *priest*, a parasitical variety of man who can exist only at the cost of every sound view of life, takes the name of God in vain: he calls that state of human society in which he himself determines the value of all things "the kingdom of God"; he calls the means whereby that state of affairs is attained "the will of God"; with cold-blooded cynicism he estimates all peoples, all ages and all individuals by the extent of their subservience or opposition to the power of the priestly order. One observes him at work: under the hand of the Jewish priesthood the *great* age of Israel became an age of decline; the Exile, with its long series of misfortunes, was transformed into a *punishment* for that great age—during which priests had not yet come into existence. Out of the powerful and *wholly free* heroes of Israel's history they fashioned, according to their changing needs, either wretched bigots and hypocrites or men entirely "godless." They reduced every great event to the idiotic formula: "obedient *or* disobedient to God."—They went a step further: the "will of God" (in other words some means necessary for preserving the power of the priests) had to be *determined*—and to this end they had to have a "revelation." In plain English, a gigantic literary fraud had to be perpetrated, and "holy scriptures" had to be concocted—and so, with the utmost hierarchical pomp, and days of penance and much lamentation over the long days of "sin" now ended, they were duly published. The "will of God," it appears, had long stood like a rock; the trouble was that mankind had neglected the "holy scriptures"... But the "will of God" had already been revealed to Moses... What happened? Simply this: the priest had formulated, once and for all time and with the strictest meticulousness, what tithes were to be paid to him, from the largest to the smallest (—not forgetting the most appetizing cuts of meat, for the priest is a great consumer of beef-steaks); in brief, he let it be known just *what he wanted*, what "the will of God" was... From this time forward things were so arranged that the priest became *indispensable everywhere*; at all the great natural events of life, at birth, at marriage, in sickness, at death, not to say at the "*sacrifice*" (that is, at meal-times), the holy parasite put in his appearance, and proceeded to *denaturize* it—in his own phrase, to "sanctify" it... For this should be noted: that every natural habit, every natural institution (the state, the administration of justice, marriage, the care of the sick and of the poor), everything demanded by the life-instinct, in short, everything that has any value *in itself*, is reduced to absolute worthlessness and even made the *reverse* of valuable by the parasitism of priests (or, if you chose, by the "moral order of the world"). The fact requires a sanction—a power to *grant values* becomes necessary, and the only way it can create such values is by denying nature... The priest depreciates and desecrates nature: it is only at this price that he can exist at all.—Disobedience to God, which actually means to the priest, to "the law," now gets the name of "sin"; the means prescribed for "reconciliation with God" are, of course, precisely the means which bring one most effectively under the thumb of the priest; he alone can "save"... Psychologically considered, "sins" are indispensable to every society organized on an ecclesiastical basis; they are the only reliable weapons of power; the priest *lives* upon sins; it is necessary to him that there be "sinning"... Prime axiom: "God forgiveth him that repenteth"—in plain English, *him that submitteth to the priest.*

27

Christianity sprang from a soil so corrupt that on it everything natural, every natural value, every *reality* was opposed by the deepest instincts of the ruling class—it grew up as a sort of war to the death upon reality, and as such it has never been surpassed. The "holy people," who had adopted priestly values and priestly names for all things, and who, with a terrible logical consistency, had rejected everything of the earth as "unholy," "worldly," "sinful"—this people put its instinct into a final formula that was logical to the point of self-annihilation: as *Christianity* it actually denied even the last form of reality, the "holy people," the "chosen people," *Jewish* reality itself. The phenomenon is of the first order of importance: the small insurrectionary movement which took the name of Jesus of Nazareth is simply the Jewish instinct *redivivus*—in other words, it is the priestly instinct come to such a pass that it can no longer endure the priest as a fact; it is the discovery of a state of existence even more fantastic than any before it, of a vision of life even more *unreal* than that necessary to an ecclesiastical organization. Christianity actually *denies* the church...

I am unable to determine what was the target of the insurrection said to have been led (whether rightly or *wrongly*) by Jesus, if it was not the Jewish church—"church" being here used in exactly the same sense that the word has today. It was an insurrection against the "good and just," against the "prophets of Israel," against the whole hierarchy of society—*not* against corruption, but against caste, privilege, order, formalism. It was *unbelief* in "superior men," a Nay flung at everything that priests and theologians stood for. But the hierarchy that was called into question, if only for an instant, by this movement was the structure of piles which, above everything, was necessary to the safety of the Jewish people in the midst of the "waters"—it represented their *last* possibility of survival; it was the final *residuum* of their independent political existence; an attack upon it was an attack upon the most profound national instinct, the most powerful national will to live, that has ever appeared on earth. This saintly anarchist, who aroused the people of the abyss, the outcasts and "sinners," the Chandala of Judaism, to rise in revolt against the established order of things—and in language which, if the Gospels are to be credited, would get him sent to Siberia today—this man was certainly a political criminal, at least in so far as it was possible to be one in so *absurdly unpolitical* a community. This is what brought him to the cross: the proof thereof is to be found in the inscription that was put upon the cross. He died for his *own* sins—there is not the slightest ground for believing, no matter how often it is asserted, that he died for the sins of others. —

28

As to whether he himself was conscious of this contradiction—whether, in fact, this was the only contradiction he was cognizant of—that is quite another question. Here, for the first time, I touch upon the problem of the *psychology of the Saviour.*—I confess, to begin with, that there are very few books which offer me harder reading than the Gospels. My difficulties are quite different from those which enabled the learned curiosity of the German mind to achieve one of its most unforgettable triumphs. It is a long while since I, like all other young scholars, enjoyed with all the sapient laboriousness of a fastidious philologist the work of the incomparable Strauss.[1] At that time I was twenty years old: now I am too serious for that sort of thing. What do I care for the contradictions of "tradition"? How can anyone call pious legends "traditions"? The histories of saints present the most dubious variety of literature in existence; to examine them by the scientific method, *in the entire absence of corroborative documents*, seems to me to condemn the whole inquiry from the start—it is simply learned idling...

29

What concerns *me* is the psychological type of the Saviour. This type might be depicted in the Gospels, in however mutilated a form and however much overladen with extraneous characters—that is, in *spite* of the Gospels; just as the figure of Francis of Assisi shows itself in his legends in spite of his legends. It is *not* a question of mere truthful evidence as to what he did, what he said and how he actually died; the question is, whether his type is still conceivable, whether it has been handed down to us.—All the attempts that I know of to read the *history* of a "soul" in the Gospels seem to me to reveal only a lamentable psychological levity. M. Renan, that mountebank *in psychologicus*, has contributed the two most *unseemly* notions to this business of explaining the type of Jesus: the notion of the *genius* and that of the *hero* ("*héros*"). But if there is anything essentially unevangelical, it is

1. David Friedrich Strauss (1808-74), author of "Das Leben Jesu" (1835-6), a very famous work in its day. Nietzsche here refers to it.

surely the concept of the hero. What the Gospels make instinctive is precisely the reverse of all heroic struggle, of all taste for conflict: the very incapacity for resistance is here converted into something moral: ("resist not evil!"—the most profound sentence in the Gospels, perhaps the true key to them), to wit, the blessedness of peace, of gentleness, the *inability* to be an enemy. What is the meaning of "glad tidings"?—The true life, the life eternal has been found—it is not merely promised, it is here, it is in *you*; it is the life that lies in love free from all retreats and exclusions, from all keeping of distances. Every one is the child of God—Jesus claims nothing for himself alone—as the child of God each man is the equal of every other man... Imagine making Jesus a *hero*!—And what a tremendous misunderstanding appears in the word "genius"! Our whole conception of the "spiritual," the whole conception of our civilization, could have had no meaning in the world that Jesus lived in. In the strict sense of the physiologist, a quite different word ought to be used here... We all know that there is a morbid sensibility of the tactile nerves which causes those suffering from it to recoil from every touch, and from every effort to grasp a solid object. Brought to its logical conclusion, such a physiological *habitus* becomes an instinctive hatred of all reality, a flight into the "intangible," into the "incomprehensible"; a distaste for all formulae, for all conceptions of time and space, for everything established—customs, institutions, the church—; a feeling of being at home in a world in which no sort of reality survives, a merely "inner" world, a "true" world, an "eternal" world... "The Kingdom of God is within *you*"...

30

The instinctive hatred of reality: the consequence of an extreme susceptibility to pain and irritation—so great that merely to be "touched" becomes unendurable, for every sensation is too profound.

The instinctive exclusion of all aversion, all hostility, all bounds and distances in feeling: the consequence of an extreme susceptibility to pain and irritation—so great that it senses all resistance, all compulsion to resistance, as unbearable *anguish* (—that is to say, as *harmful*, as *prohibited* by the instinct of self-preservation), and regards blessedness (joy) as possible only when it is no longer necessary to offer resistance to anybody or anything, however evil or dangerous—love, as the only, as the *ultimate* possibility of life...

These are the two *physiological realities* upon and out of which the doctrine of salvation has sprung. I call them a sublime super-development of hedonism upon a thoroughly unsalubrious soil. What stands most closely related to them, though with a large admixture of Greek vitality and nerve-force, is epicureanism, the theory of salvation of paganism. Epicurus was a *typical décadent*: I was the first to recognize him.—The fear of pain, even of infinitely slight pain—the end of this *can* be nothing save a *religion of love*...

31

I have already given my answer to the problem. The prerequisite to it is the assumption that the type of the Saviour has reached us only in a greatly distorted form. This distortion is very probable:

there are many reasons why a type of that sort should not be handed down in a pure form, complete and free of additions. The milieu in which this strange figure moved must have left marks upon him, and more must have been imprinted by the history, the *destiny*, of the early Christian communities; the latter indeed, must have embellished the type retrospectively with characters which can be understood only as serving the purposes of war and of propaganda. That strange and sickly world into which the Gospels lead us—a world apparently out of a Russian novel, in which the scum of society, nervous maladies and "childish" idiocy keep a tryst—must, in any case, have *coarsened* the type: the first disciples, in particular, must have been forced to translate an existence visible only in symbols and incomprehensibilities into their own crudity, in order to understand it at all—in their sight the type could take on reality only after it had been recast in a familiar mould... The prophet, the messiah, the future judge, the teacher of morals, the worker of wonders, John the Baptist—all these merely presented chances to misunderstand it... Finally, let us not underrate the *proprium* of all great, and especially all sectarian veneration: it tends to erase from the venerated objects all its original traits and idiosyncrasies, often so painfully strange—*it does not even see them*. It is greatly to be regretted that no Dostoyevsky lived in the neighbourhood of this most interesting *décadent*—I mean someone who would have felt the poignant charm of such a compound of the sublime, the morbid and the childish. In the last analysis, the type, as a type of the *décadence*, may actually have been peculiarly complex and contradictory: such a possibility is not to be lost sight of. Nevertheless, the probabilities seem to be against it, for in that case tradition would have been particularly accurate and objective, whereas we have reasons for assuming the contrary.

Meanwhile, there is a contradiction between the peaceful preacher of the mount, the sea-shore and the fields, who appears like a new Buddha on a soil very unlike India's, and the aggressive fanatic, the mortal enemy of theologians and ecclesiastics, who stands glorified by Renan's malice as "*le grand maître en ironie.*" I myself haven't any doubt that the greater part of this venom (and no less of *esprit*) got itself into the concept of the Master only as a result of the excited nature of Christian propaganda: we all know the unscrupulousness of sectarians when they set out to turn their leader into an *apologia* for themselves. When the early Christians had need of an adroit, contentious, pugnacious and maliciously subtle theologian to tackle other theologians, they *created* a "god" that met that need, just as they put into his mouth without hesitation certain ideas that were necessary to them but that were utterly at odds with the Gospels—"the second coming," "the last judgment," all sorts of expectations and promises, current at the time.—

32

I can only repeat that I set myself against all efforts to intrude the fanatic into the figure of the Saviour: the very word *impérieux*, used by Renan, is alone enough to *annul* the type. What the "glad tidings" tell us is simply that there are no more contradictions; the kingdom of heaven belongs to *children*; the faith that is voiced here is no more an embattled faith—it is at hand, it has been from the beginning, it is a sort of recrudescent childishness of the spirit. The physiologists, at all events, are familiar with such a delayed and incomplete puberty in the living organism, the result of degeneration. A faith of this sort is not furious, it does not de nounce, it does not defend itself: it does not come with "the sword"—it does not realize how it will one day set man against man. It does not manifest itself either by miracles, or by rewards and promises, or by "scriptures": it is itself, first and last, its own miracle, its own reward, its own promise, its own "kingdom of God." This faith does not formulate itself—it simply *lives*, and so guards itself against formulae. To be sure, the accident of environment, of educational background gives prominence to concepts of a certain sort: in primitive Christianity one finds *only* concepts of a Judaeo-Semitic character (—that of eating and drinking at the last supper belongs to this category—an idea which, like everything else Jewish, has been badly mauled by the church). But let us be careful not to see in all this anything more than symbolical language, semantics[1] an opportunity to speak in parables. It is only on the theory that no work is to be taken literally that this anti-realist is able to speak at all. Set down among Hindus he would have made use of the concepts of Sankhya,[2] and among Chinese he would have employed those of Lao-tse[3]—and in neither case would it have made any difference to him.—With a little freedom in the use of words, one might actually call Jesus a "free spirit"[4]—he cares nothing for what is established: the word *killeth*,[5] whatever is established *killeth*. The idea of "life" as an *experience*, as he alone conceives it, stands opposed to his mind to every sort of word, formula, law, belief and dogma. He speaks only of inner things: "life" or "truth" or "light" is his word for the innermost—in his sight everything else, the whole of reality, all nature, even language, has significance

1. The word *Semiotik* is in the text, but it is probable that *Semantik* is what Nietzsche had in mind.
2. One of the six great systems of Hindu philosophy.
3. The reputed founder of Taoism.
4. Nietzsche's name for one accepting his own philosophy.
5. That is, the strict letter of the law—the chief target of Jesus's early preaching.

only as sign, as allegory.—Here it is of paramount importance to be led into no error by the temptations lying in Christian, or rather *ecclesiastical* prejudices: such a symbolism *par excellence* stands outside all religion, all notions of worship, all history, all natural science, all worldly experience, all knowledge, all politics, all psychology, all books, all art—his "wisdom" is precisely a *pure ignorance*[1] of all such things. He has never heard of *culture*; he doesn't have to make war on it—he doesn't even deny it... The same thing may be said of the *state*, of the whole bourgeoise social order, of labour, of war—he has no ground for denying "the world," for he knows nothing of the ecclesiastical concept of "the world"... *Denial* is precisely the thing that is impossible to him.—In the same way he lacks argumentative capacity, and has no belief that an article of faith, a "truth," may be established by proofs (—*his* proofs are inner "lights," subjective sensations of happiness and self-approval, simple "proofs of power"—). Such a doctrine *cannot* contradict: it doesn't know that other doctrines exist, or *can* exist, and is wholly incapable of imagining anything opposed to it... If anything of the sort is ever encountered, it laments the "blindness" with sincere sympathy—for it alone has "light"—but it does not offer objections...

33

In the whole psychology of the "Gospels" the concepts of guilt and punishment are lacking, and so is that of reward. "Sin," which means anything that puts a distance between God and man, is abolished—*this is precisely the "glad tidings."* Eternal bliss is not merely promised, nor is it bound up with conditions: it is

1. A reference to the "pure ignorance" (*reine Thorheit*) of Parsifal.

conceived as the *only* reality—what remains consists merely of signs useful in speaking of it.

The *results* of such a point of view project themselves into a new *way of life*, the special evangelical way of life. It is not a "belief" that marks off the Christian; he is distinguished by a different mode of action; he acts *differently*. He offers no resistance, either by word or in his heart, to those who stand against him. He draws no distinction between strangers and countrymen, Jews and Gentiles ("neighbour," of course, means fellow-believer, Jew). He is angry with no one, and he despises no one. He neither appeals to the courts of justice nor heeds their mandates ("Swear not at all").[1] He never under any circumstances divorces his wife, even when he has proofs of her infidelity.—And under all of this is one principle; all of it arises from one instinct.—

The life of the Saviour was simply a carrying out of this way of life—and so was his death... He no longer needed any formula or ritual in his relations with God—not even prayer. He had rejected the whole of the Jewish doctrine of repentance and atonement; he *knew* that it was only by a *way* of life that one could feel one's self "divine," "blessed," "evangelical," a "child of God." *Not* by "repentance," *not* by "prayer and forgiveness" is the way to God: *only the Gospel way* leads to God—it is *itself* "God!"—What the Gospels *abolished* was the Judaism in the concepts of "sin," "forgiveness of sin," "faith," "salvation through faith"—the whole *ecclesiastical* dogma of the Jews was denied by the "glad tidings."

The deep instinct which prompts the Christian how to *live* so that he will feel that he is "in heaven" and is "immortal," despite many reasons for feeling that he is *not* "in heaven": this is the only

1. Matthew v, 34.

psychological reality in "salvation."—A new way of life, *not* a new faith...

34

If I understand anything at all about this great symbolist, it is this: that he regarded only *subjective* realities as realities, as "truths" —that he saw everything else, everything natural, temporal, spatial and historical, merely as signs, as materials for parables. The concept of "the Son of God" does not connote a concrete person in history, an isolated and definite individual, but an "eternal" fact, a psychological symbol set free from the concept of time. The same thing is true, and in the highest sense, of the *God* of this typical symbolist, of the "kingdom of God," and of the "sonship of God." Nothing could be more un-Christian than the *crude ecclesiastical* notions of God as a *person*, of a "kingdom of God" that is to come, of a "kingdom of heaven" beyond, and of a "son of God" as the *second person* of the Trinity. All this—if I may be forgiven the phrase—is like thrusting one's fist into the eye (and what an eye!) of the Gospels: a disrespect for symbols amounting to *world-historical cynicism*... But it is nevertheless obvious enough what is meant by the symbols "Father" and "Son"—not, of course, to every one—: the word "Son" expresses *entrance* into the feeling that there is a general transformation of all things (beatitude), and "Father" expresses *that feeling itself*—the sensation of eternity and of perfection.—I am ashamed to remind you of what the church has made of this symbolism: has it not set an Amphitryon story[1] at the threshold

1. Amphitryon was the son of Alcaeus, King of Tiryns. His wife was Alcmene. During his absence she was visited by Zeus, and bore Heracles.

of the Christian "faith"? And a dogma of "immaculate conception" for good measure?... *And thereby it has robbed conception of its immaculateness*—

The "kingdom of heaven" is a state of the heart—not something to come "beyond the world" or "after death." The whole idea of natural death is *absent* from the Gospels: death is not a bridge, not a passing; it is absent because it belongs to a quite different, a merely apparent world, useful only as a symbol. The "hour of death" is *not* a Christian idea—"hours," time, the physical life and its crises have no existence for the bearer of "glad tidings."... The "kingdom of God" is not something that men wait for: it had no yesterday and no day after tomorrow, it is not going to come at a "millennium"—it is an experience of the heart, it is everywhere and it is nowhere...

35

This "bearer of glad tidings" died as he lived and *taught—not* to "save mankind," but to show mankind how to live. It was a *way of life* that he bequeathed to man: his demeanour before the judges, before the officers, before his accusers—his demeanour on the *cross*. He does not resist; he does not defend his rights; he makes no effort to ward off the most extreme penalty—more, *he invites it*... And he prays, suffers and loves *with* those, *in* those, who do him evil... *Not* to defend one's self, *not* to show anger, *not* to lay blames... On the contrary, to submit even to the Evil One—to *love* him...

36

—We free spirits—we are the first to have the necessary prerequisite to understanding what nineteen centuries have misunderstood—that instinct and passion for integrity which makes war upon the "holy lie" even more than upon all other lies... Mankind was unspeakably far from our benevolent and cautious neutrality, from that discipline of the spirit which alone makes possible the solution of such strange and subtle things: what men always sought, with shameless egoism, was their *own* advantage therein; they created the *church* out of denial of the Gospels...

Whoever sought for signs of an ironical divinity's hand in the great drama of existence would find no small indication thereof in the *stupendous question-mark* that is called Christianity. That mankind should be on its knees before the very antithesis of what was the origin, the meaning and the *law* of the Gospels—that in the concept of the "church" the very things should be pronounced holy that the "bearer of glad tidings" regards as *beneath* him and *behind* him—it would be impossible to surpass this as a grand example of *world-historical irony*—

37

—Our age is proud of its historical sense: how, then, could it delude itself into believing that the *crude fable of the wonder-worker and Saviour* constituted the beginnings of Christianity—and that everything spiritual and symbolical in it only came later? Quite to the contrary, the whole history of Christianity—from the death on the cross onward—is the history of a progressively clumsier misunderstanding of an *original* symbolism. With every extension of Christianity among larger and ruder masses, even less capable of grasping the principles that gave birth to it, the need arose to make it more and more *vulgar* and *barbarous*—it absorbed the teachings and rites of all the *subterranean* cults of the *imperium Romanum*, and the absurdities engendered by all sorts of sickly reasoning. It was the fate of Christianity that its faith had to become as sickly, as low and as vulgar as the needs were sickly, low and vulgar to which it had to administer. A *sickly barbarism* finally lifts itself to power as the church—the church, that incarnation of deadly hostility to all honesty, to all loftiness of soul, to all discipline of the spirit, to all spontaneous and kindly humanity.—*Christian* values—*noble* values: it is only we, we *free* spirits, who have re-established this greatest of all antitheses in values!...

38

—I cannot, at this place, avoid a sigh. There are days when I am visited by a feeling blacker than the blackest melancholy—*contempt of man*. Let me leave no doubt as to *what* I despise, *whom* I despise: it is the man of today, the man with whom I am unhappily contemporaneous. The man of today—I am suffocated by his foul breath!... Toward the past, like all who understand, I am full of tolerance, which is to say, *generous* self-control: with gloomy caution I pass through whole millenniums of this madhouse of a world, call it "Christianity," "Christian faith" or the "Christian church," as you will—I take care not to hold mankind responsible for its lunacies. But my feeling changes and breaks out irresistibly the moment I enter modern times, *our* times. Our age *knows better*... What was formerly merely sickly now becomes indecent—it is indecent to be a Christian today. *And here my disgust begins.*—I look about me: not a word survives of what was once called "truth"; we can no longer bear to hear a priest pronounce the word. Even a man who makes the most modest pretensions to integrity *must* know that a theologian, a priest, a pope of today not only errs when he speaks, but actually *lies*—and that he no longer escapes blame for his lie through "innocence" or "ignorance." The priest knows, as everyone knows, that there is no longer any "God," or any "sinner," or any "Saviour"—that "free will" and the "moral order of the world" are lies—: serious reflection, the profound self-conquest of the spirit, *allow* no man to pretend that he does *not* know it... *All* the ideas of the church are now recognized for what they are—as the worst counterfeits in existence, invented to debase nature and all natural values; the priest himself is seen as he actually is—as the most dangerous form of parasite, as the venomous spider of creation... We know, our *conscience* now knows—just *what* the real value of all those sinister inventions of priest and church has been and *what ends they have served*, with their debasement of humanity to a state of self-pollution, the very sight of which excites loathing,—the concepts "the other world," "the last judgment," "the immortality of the soul," the "soul" itself: they are all merely so many instruments of torture, systems of cruelty, whereby the priest becomes master and remains master... Everyone knows this, *but nevertheless things remain as before*. What has become of the last trace of decent feeling, of self-respect, when our statesmen, otherwise an unconventional class of men and thoroughly anti-Christian in their acts, now call themselves Christians and go to the communion-table?... A prince at the head of his armies, magnificent as the expression of the egoism and arrogance of his people—and yet acknowledging, *without* any shame, that he is a Christian!... Whom, then, does Christianity deny? *what* does it call "the world"? To be a *soldier*, to be a judge, to be a patriot; to defend one's self; to be careful of one's honour; to desire one's own advantage; to be *proud*... every act of every day, every instinct, every valuation that shows itself in a *deed*, is now anti-Christian: what a *monster of falsehood* the modern man must be to call himself nevertheless, and *without* shame, a Christian!—

39

—I shall go back a bit, and tell you the *authentic* history of Christianity.—The very word "Christianity" is a misunderstanding—at bottom there was only one Christian, and he died on the cross. The "Gospels" *died* on the cross. What, from that moment onward, was called the "Gospels" was the very reverse of what *he* had lived: "bad tidings," a *Dysangelium*.[1] It is an error amounting to nonsensicality to see in "faith," and particularly in faith in salvation through Christ, the distinguishing mark of the Christian: only the Christian *way of life*, the life *lived* by him who died on the cross, is Christian... To this day *such* a life is still possible, and for *certain* men even necessary: genuine, primitive Christianity will remain possible in all ages... *Not* faith, but acts; above all, an *avoidance* of acts, a different *state of being*... States of consciousness, faith of a sort, the acceptance, for example, of anything as true—as every psychologist knows, the value of these things is perfectly indifferent and fifth-rate compared to that of the instincts: strictly speaking, the whole concept of intellectual causality is false. To reduce being a Christian, the state

1. So in the text. One of Nietzsche's numerous coinages, obviously suggested by *Evangelium*, the German for *gospel*.

of Christianity, to an acceptance of truth, to a mere phenomenon of consciousness, is to formulate the negation of Christianity. *In fact, there are no Christians.* The "Christian"—he who for two thousand years has passed as a Christian—is simply a psycho logical self-delusion. Closely examined, it appears that, *despite* all his "faith," he has been ruled *only* by his instincts—and *what instincts*!—In all ages—for example, in the case of Luther—"faith" has been no more than a cloak, a pretense, a *curtain* behind which the instincts have played their game—a shrewd *blindness* to the domination of *certain* of the instincts... I have already called "faith" the specially Christian form of *shrewdness*—people always *talk* of their "faith" and *act* according to their instincts... In the world of ideas of the Christian there is nothing that so much as touches reality: on the contrary, one recognizes an instinctive *hatred* of reality as the motive power, the only motive power at the bottom of Christianity. What follows there from? That even here, in *psychologicis*, there is a radical error, which is to say one conditioning fundamentals, which is to say, one in *substance.* Take away one idea and put a genuine reality in its place—and the whole of Christianity crumbles to nothingness!—Viewed calmly, this strangest of all phenomena, a religion not only depending on errors, but inventive and ingenious *only* in devising injurious errors, poisonous to life and to the heart—this remains a *spectacle for the gods*—for those gods who are also philosophers, and whom I have encountered, for example, in the celebrated dialogues at Naxos. At the moment when their *disgust* leaves them (—and us!) they will be thankful for the spectacle afforded by the Christians: perhaps because of *this* curious exhibition alone the wretched little planet called the earth deserves a glance from omnipotence, a show of divine interest... Therefore, let us not underestimate the Christians: the Christian, false *to the point of innocence*, is far above the ape—in its application to the Christians a well-known theory of descent becomes a mere piece of politeness...

40

—The fate of the Gospels was decided by death—it hung on the "cross."... It was only death, that unexpected and shameful death; it was only the cross, which was usually reserved for the canaille only—it was only this appalling paradox which brought the disciples face to face with the real riddle: "*Who was it? what was it?*"—The feeling of dis may, of profound affront and injury; the suspicion that such a death might involve a *refutation* of their cause; the terrible question, "Why just in this way?"—this state of mind is only too easy to understand. Here everything *must* be accounted for as necessary; everything must have a meaning, a reason, the highest sort of reason; the love of a disciple excludes all chance. Only then did the chasm of doubt yawn: "*Who* put him to death? who was his natural enemy?"—this question flashed like a lightning-stroke. Answer: dominant Judaism, its ruling class. From that moment, one found one's self in revolt *against* the established order, and began to understand Jesus as *in revolt against the established order*. Until then this militant, this nay-saying, nay-doing element in his character had been lacking; what is more, he had appeared to present its opposite. Obviously, the little community had *not* understood what was precisely the most important thing of all: the example offered by this way of dying, the freedom from and superiority to every feeling of *ressentiment*—a plain indication of how little he was understood at all! All that Jesus could hope to accomplish by his death, in itself, was to offer the strongest possible proof, for *example*, of his teachings in the most public manner... But his disciples were very far from *forgiving* his death—though to have done so would have accorded with the Gospels in the highest degree; and neither were they prepared to *offer* themselves, with gentle and serene calmness of heart, for a similar death... On the contrary, it was precisely the most unevangelical of feelings, *revenge*, that now possessed them. It seemed impossible that the cause should perish with his death: "recompense" and "judgment" became necessary (—yet what could be less evangelical than "recompense," "punishment," and "sitting in judgment"!). Once more the popular belief in the coming of a messiah appeared in the foreground; attention was rivetted upon an historical moment: the "kingdom of God" is to come, with judgment upon his enemies... But in all this there was a wholesale misunderstanding: imagine the "kingdom of God" as a last act, as a mere promise! The Gospels had been, in fact, the incarnation, the fulfilment, the *realization* of this "kingdom of God." It was only now that all the familiar contempt for and bitterness against Pharisees and theologians began to appear in the character of the Master—he was thereby *turned* into a Pharisee and theologian himself! On the other hand, the savage veneration of these completely unbalanced souls could no longer endure the Gospel doctrine, taught by Jesus, of the equal right of all men to be children of God: their revenge took the form of *elevating* Jesus in an extravagant fashion, and thus separating him from themselves: just as, in earlier times, the Jews, to revenge themselves upon their enemies, separated themselves from their God, and placed him on a great height. The One God and the Only Son of God: both were products of *ressentiment*...

41

—And from that time onward an absurd problem offered itself: "how *could* God allow it!" To which the deranged reason of the little community formulated an answer that was terrifying in its absurdity: God gave his son as a *sacrifice* for the forgiveness of sins. At once there was an end of the gospels! Sacrifice for sin, and in its most obnoxious and barbarous form: sacrifice of the *innocent* for the sins of the guilty! What appalling paganism!—Jesus himself had done away with the very concept of "guilt," he denied that there was any gulf fixed between God and man; he *lived* this unity between God and man, and that was precisely *his* "glad tidings"... And *not* as a mere privilege!—From this time forward the type of the Saviour was corrupted, bit by bit, by the doctrine of judgment and of the second coming, the doctrine of death as a sacrifice, the doctrine of the *resurrection*, by means of which the entire concept of "blessedness," the whole and only reality of the gospels, is juggled away—in favour of a state of existence *after* death!... St. Paul, with that rabbinical impudence which shows itself in all his doings, gave a logical quality to that conception, that *indecent* conception, in this way: "*If* Christ did not rise from the dead, then all our faith is in vain!"—And at once there sprang from the Gospels the most contemptible of all unfulfillable promises, the *shameless* doctrine of personal immortality... Paul even preached it as a *reward*...

42

One now begins to see just *what* it was that came to an end with the death on the cross: a new and thoroughly original effort to found a Buddhistic peace movement, and so establish *happiness on earth*—real, *not* merely promised. For this remains—as I have already pointed out—the essential difference between the two religions of *décadence*: Buddhism promises nothing, but actually fulfils; Christianity promises everything, but *fulfils nothing*.—Hard upon the heels of the "glad tidings" came the worst imaginable: those of Paul. In Paul is incarnated the very opposite of the "bearer of glad tidings"; he represents the genius for hatred, the vision of hatred, the relentless logic of hatred. *What*, indeed, has not this dysangelist sacrificed to hatred! Above all, the Saviour: he nailed him to *his own* cross. The life, the example, the teaching, the death of Christ, the meaning and the law of the whole gospels—nothing was left of all this after that counterfeiter in hatred had reduced it to his uses. Surely *not* reality; surely *not* historical truth!... Once more the priestly instinct of the Jew perpetrated the same old master crime against history—he simply struck out the yesterday and the day before yesterday of Christianity, and *invented his own history of Christian beginnings*. Going further, he treated the history of Israel to another falsification, so that it became a mere prologue to *his* achievement: all the prophets, it now appeared, had referred to *his* "Saviour."... Later on the church even falsified the history of man in order to make it a prologue to Christianity... The figure of the Saviour, his teaching, his way of life, his death, the meaning of his death, even the consequences of his death—nothing remained untouched, nothing remained in even remote contact with reality. Paul simply shifted the centre of gravity of that whole life to a place *behind* this existence—in the *lie* of the "risen" Jesus. At bottom, he had no use for the life of the Saviour—what he needed was the death on the cross, *and* something more. To see anything honest in such a man as Paul, whose home was at the centre of the Stoical enlightenment, when he converts an hallucination into a *proof* of the resurrection of the Saviour, or even to believe his tale that he suffered from this hallucination himself—this would be a genuine *niaiserie* in a psychologist. Paul willed the end; *therefore* he also willed the means... What he himself didn't believe was swallowed readily enough by the idiots among whom he spread *his* teaching.—What *he* wanted was power; in Paul the priest once more reached out for power—he had use only for such concepts, teachings and symbols as served the purpose of tyrannizing over the masses and organizing mobs. *What* was the only part of Christianity that Mohammed borrowed later on? Paul's invention, his device for establishing priestly tyranny and organizing the mob: the belief in the immortality of the soul—*that is to say, the doctrine of "judgment"*...

43

When the centre of gravity of life is placed, *not* in life itself, but in "the beyond"—in *nothingness*—then one has taken away its centre of gravity altogether. The vast lie of personal immortality destroys all reason, all natural instinct—henceforth, everything in the instincts that is beneficial, that fosters life and that safeguards the future is a cause of suspicion. So to live that life no longer has any meaning: *this* is now the "meaning" of life... Why be public-spirited? Why take any pride in descent and forefathers? Why labour together, trust one another, or concern one's self about the common welfare, and try to serve it?... Merely so many "temptations," so many strayings from the "straight path."—"*One* thing only is necessary"... That every man, because he has an "immortal soul," is as good as every other man; that in an infinite universe of things the "salvation" of *every* individual may lay claim to eternal importance; that insignificant bigots and the three-fourths insane may assume that the laws of nature are constantly *suspended* in their behalf—it is impossible to lavish too much contempt upon such a magnification of every sort of selfishness to infinity, to *insolence*. And yet Christianity has to thank precisely *this* miserable flattery of personal vanity for its *triumph*—it was thus that it lured all the botched, the dissatisfied, the fallen upon evil days, the whole refuse and off-scouring of humanity to its side. The "salvation of the soul"—in plain English: "the world revolves around *me*."... The poisonous doctrine, "*equal* rights for all," has been propagated as a Christian principle: out of the secret nooks and crannies of bad instinct Christianity has waged a deadly war upon all feelings of reverence and distance between man and man, which is to say, upon the first *prerequisite* to every step upward, to every development of civilization—out of the *ressentiment* of the masses it has forged its chief weapons against *us*, against everything noble, joyous and high-spirited on earth, against our happiness on earth... To allow "immortality" to every Peter and Paul was the greatest, the most vicious outrage upon *noble* humanity ever perpetrated.—*And* let us not underestimate the fatal influence that Christianity has had, even upon politics! Nowadays no one has courage any more for special rights, for the right of dominion, for feelings of honourable pride in himself and his equals—for the *pathos of distance*... Our politics is sick with this lack of courage!—The aristocratic attitude of mind has been undermined by the lie of the equality of souls; and if belief in the "privileges of the majority" makes and *will continue to make* revolutions—it is Christianity, let us not doubt, and *Christian* valuations, which convert every revolution into a carnival of blood and crime! Christianity is a revolt of all creatures that creep on the ground against everything that is *lofty*: the gospel of the "lowly" *lowers*...

44

—The gospels are invaluable as evidence of the corruption that was already persistent *within* the primitive community. That which Paul, with the cynical logic of a rabbi, later developed to a conclusion was at bottom merely a process of decay that had begun with the death of the Saviour.—These gospels cannot be read too carefully; difficulties lurk behind every word. I confess—I hope it will not be held against me—that it is precisely for this reason that they offer first-rate joy to a psychologist—as the *opposite* of all merely naïve corruption, as refinement *par excellence*, as an artistic triumph in psychological corruption. The gospels, in fact, stand alone. The Bible as a whole is not to be compared to them. Here we are among Jews: this is the *first* thing to be borne in mind if we are not to lose the thread of the matter. This positive genius for conjuring up a delusion of personal "holiness" unmatched anywhere else, either in books or by men; this elevation of fraud in word and attitude to the level of an *art*—all this is not an accident due to the chance talents of an individual, or to any violation of nature. The thing responsible is *race*. The whole of Judaism appears in Christianity as the art of concocting holy lies, and there, after many centuries of earnest Jewish training and hard practice of Jewish technic, the business comes to the stage of mastery. The Christian, that *ultima ratio* of lying, is the Jew all over again—he is *threefold* the Jew... The underlying will to make use only of such concepts, symbols and attitudes as fit into priestly practice, the instinctive repudiation of every *other* mode of thought, and every other method of estimating values and utilities—this is not only tradition, it is *inheritance*: only as an inheritance is it able to operate with the force of nature. The whole of mankind, even the best minds of the best ages (with one exception, perhaps hardly human—), have permitted themselves to be deceived. The gospels have been read as a *book of innocence*... surely no small indication of the high skill with which the trick has been done.—Of course, if we could actually *see* these astounding bigots and bogus saints, even if only for an instant, the farce would come to an end,—and it is precisely because *I* cannot read a word of theirs without seeing their attitudinizing that *I have made an end of them*... I simply cannot endure the way they have of rolling up their eyes.—For the majority, happily enough, books are mere *literature*.—Let us not be led astray: they say "judge not," and yet they condemn to hell whoever stands in their way. In letting God sit in judgment they judge themselves; in glorifying God they glorify themselves; in *demanding* that every one show the virtues which they themselves happen to be capable of—still more, which they *must* have in order to remain on top—they assume the grand air of men struggling for virtue, of men engaging in a war that virtue may prevail. "We live, we die, we sacrifice ourselves *for the good*" (—"the truth," "the light," "the kingdom of God"): in point of fact, they simply do what they cannot help doing. Forced, like hypocrites, to be sneaky, to hide in corners, to slink along in the shadows, they convert their necessity into a *duty*: it is on grounds of duty that they account for their lives of humility, and that humility becomes merely one more proof of their piety... Ah, that humble, chaste, charitable brand of fraud! "Virtue itself shall bear witness for us."... One may read the gospels as books of *moral* seduction: these petty folks fasten themselves to morality—they know the uses of morality! Morality is the best of all devices for leading mankind *by the nose*!—The fact is that the conscious conceit of the chosen here disguises itself as modesty: it is in this way that *they*, the "community," the "good and just," range themselves, once and for always, on one side, the side of "the truth"—and the rest of mankind, "the world," on the other... In *that* we observe the most fatal sort of megalomania that the earth has ever seen: little abortions of bigots and liars began to claim exclusive rights in the concepts of "God," "the truth," "the light," "the spirit," "love," "wisdom" and "life," as if these things were synonyms of themselves and thereby they sought to fence themselves off from the "world"; little super-Jews, ripe for some sort of madhouse, turned values upside down in order to meet *their* notions, just as if the Christian were the meaning, the salt, the standard and even the *last judgment* of all the rest... The whole disaster was only made possible by the fact that there already existed in the world a similar megalomania, allied to this one in race, to wit, the *Jewish*: once a chasm began to yawn between Jews and Judaeo-Christians, the latter had no choice but to employ the self-preservative measures that the Jewish instinct had devised, even *against* the Jews themselves, whereas the Jews had employed them only against non-Jews. The Christian is simply a Jew of the "reformed" confession.—

45

—I offer a few examples of the sort of thing these petty people have got into their heads—what they have *put into the mouth* of the Master: the unalloyed creed of "beautiful souls."—

"And whosoever shall not receive you, nor hear you, when ye depart thence, shake off the dust under your feet for a testimony against them. Verily I say unto you, it shall be more tolerable for Sodom and Gomorrha in the day of judgment, than for that city" (Mark vi, 11)—How *evangelical*!...

"And whosoever shall offend one of *these* little ones that believe in me, it is better for him that a millstone were hanged about his neck, and he were cast into the sea" (Mark ix, 42).—How *evangelical*!...

"And if thine eye offend thee, pluck it out: it is better for thee to enter into the kingdom of God with one eye, than having two eyes to be cast into hell fire; Where the worm dieth not, and the fire is not quenched." (Mark ix, 47.[1])—It is not exactly the eye that is meant...

"Verily I say unto you, That there be some of them that stand here, which shall not taste of death, till they have seen the kingdom of God come with power." (Mark ix, 1.)—Well *lied*, lion![2]...

"Whosoever will come after me, let him deny himself, and take up his cross, and follow me. *For...*" (*Note of a psychologist.* Christian morality is refuted by its *fors*: its reasons are against it,—this makes it Christian.) Mark viii, 34.—

"Judge not, that ye be not judged. With what measure ye mete, it shall be measured to you again." (Matthew vii, 1.[3])—What a notion of justice, of a "just" judge!...

"For if ye love them which love you, what reward have ye? do not even the publicans the same? And if ye salute your brethren only, what do ye more *than others*? do not even the publicans so?"

---

1. To which, without mentioning it, Nietzsche adds verse 48.
2. A paraphrase of Demetrius' "Well roar'd, Lion!" in act v, scene 1 of "A Midsummer Night's Dream." The lion, of course, is the familiar Christian symbol for Mark.
3. Nietzsche also quotes part of verse 2.

(Matthew v, 46.[1])—Principle of "Christian love": it insists upon being well *paid* in the end...

"But if ye forgive not men their trespasses, neither will your Father forgive your trespasses." (Matthew vi, 15.)—Very compromising for the said "father."...

"But seek ye first the kingdom of God, and his righteousness; and all these things shall be added unto you." (Matthew vi, 33.)—All these things: namely, food, clothing, all the necessities of life. An *error*, to put it mildly... A bit before this God appears as a tailor, at least in certain cases...

"Rejoice ye in that day, and leap for joy: for, behold, your reward *is* great in heaven: for in the like manner did their fathers unto the prophets." (Luke vi, 23.)—*Impudent* rabble! It compares itself to the prophets...

"Know ye not that ye are the temple of God, and *that* the spirit of God dwelleth in you? If any man defile the temple of God, *him shall God destroy*; for the temple of God is holy, *which temple ye are*." (Paul, 1 Corinthians iii, 16.[2])—For that sort of thing one cannot have enough contempt...

"Do ye not know that the saints shall judge the world? and if the world shall be judged by you, are ye unworthy to judge the smallest matters?" (Paul, 1 Corinthians vi, 2.)—Unfortunately, not merely the speech of a lunatic... This *frightful impostor* then proceeds: "Know ye not that we shall judge angels? how much more things that pertain to this life?"...

"Hath not God made foolish the wisdom of this world? For after that in the wisdom of God the world by wisdom knew not God, it pleased God by the foolishness of preaching to save

1. The quotation also includes verse 47.
2. And 17.

them that believe... Not many wise men after the flesh, not men mighty, not many noble *are called*: But God hath chosen the foolish things of the world to confound the wise; and God hath chosen the weak things of the world to confound the things which are mighty; And base things of the world, and things which are despised, hath God chosen, *yea*, and things which are not, to bring to nought things that are: That no flesh should glory in his presence." (Paul, 1 Corinthians i, 20ff.[1])—In order to *understand* this passage, a first-rate example of the psychology underlying every Chandala-morality, one should read the first part of my "Genealogy of Morals": there, for the first time, the antagonism between a *noble* morality and a morality born of *ressentiment* and impotent vengefulness is exhibited. Paul was the greatest of all apostles of revenge...

46

—*What follows, then?* That one had better put on gloves before reading the New Testament. The presence of so much filth makes it very advisable. One would as little choose "early Christians" for companions as Polish Jews: not that one need seek out an objection to them... Neither has a pleasant smell.—I have searched the New Testament in vain for a single sympathetic touch; nothing is there that is free, kindly, open-hearted or upright. In it humanity does not even make the first step upward—the instinct for *cleanliness* is lacking... Only *evil* instincts are there, and there is not even the courage of these evil instincts. It is all coward ice; it is all a shutting of the eyes, a self-deception. Every other book becomes clean, once one has read the New Testament: for example, immediately

1. Verses 20, 21, 26, 27, 28, 29.

after reading Paul I took up with delight that most charming and wanton of scoffers, Petronius, of whom one may say what Domenico Boccaccio wrote of Cæsar Borgia to the Duke of Parma: "*è tutto festo*"—immortally healthy, immortally cheerful and sound... These petty bigots make a capital miscalculation. They attack, but everything they attack is thereby *distinguished.* Whoever is attacked by an "early Christian" is surely *not* befouled... On the contrary, it is an honour to have an "early Christian" as an opponent. One cannot read the New Testament without acquired admiration for whatever it abuses—not to speak of the "wisdom of this world," which an impudent windbag tries to dispose of "by the foolishness of preaching."... Even the scribes and pharisees are benefitted by such opposition: they must certainly have been worth something to have been hated in such an indecent manner. Hypocrisy—as if this were a charge that the "early Christians" *dared* to make!—After all, they were the *privileged*, and that was enough: the hatred of the Chandala needed no other excuse. The "early Christian"—and also, I fear, the "last Christian," *whom I may perhaps live to see*—is a rebel against all privilege by profound instinct—he lives and makes war for ever for "equal rights."... Strictly speaking, he has no alternative. When a man proposes to represent, in his own person, the "chosen of God"—or to be a "temple of God," or a "judge of the angels"—then every *other* criterion, whether based upon honesty, upon intellect, upon manliness and pride, or upon beauty and freedom of the heart, becomes simply "worldly"—*evil in itself*... Moral: every word that comes from the lips of an "early Christian" is a lie, and his every act is instinctively dishonest—all his values, all his aims are noxious, but *whoever* he hates, *whatever* he hates, has real *value*... The Christian, and particularly the Christian priest, is thus a *criterion of values.*

—Must I add that, in the whole New Testament, there appears but a *solitary* figure worthy of honour? Pilate, the Roman viceroy. To regard a Jewish imbroglio *seriously*—that was quite beyond him. One Jew more or less—what did it matter?... The noble scorn of a Roman, before whom the word "truth" was shamelessly mishandled, enriched the New Testament with the only saying *that has any value*—and that is at once its criticism and its *destruction*: "What is truth?..."

47

—The thing that sets us apart is not that we are unable to find God, either in history, or in nature, or behind nature—but that we regard what has been honoured as God, not as "divine," but as pitiable, as absurd, as injurious; not as a mere error, but as a *crime against life*... We deny that God is God... If any one were to *show* us this Christian God, we'd be still less inclined to believe in him.—In a formula: *deus, qualem Paulus creavit, dei negatio.*—Such a religion as Christianity, which does not touch reality at a single point and which goes to pieces the moment reality asserts its rights at any point, must be inevitably the deadly enemy of the "wisdom of this world," which is to say, of *science*—and it will give the name of good to whatever means serve to poison, calumniate and *cry down* all intellectual discipline, all lucidity and strictness in matters of intellectual conscience, and all noble coolness and freedom of the mind. "Faith," as an imperative, vetoes science—*in praxi*, lying at any price... Paul *well knew* that lying—that "faith"—was necessary; later on the church borrowed the fact from Paul.—The God that Paul invented for himself, a God who "reduced to absurdity" "the wisdom of this world" (especially the two great enemies of superstition, philology and medicine), is in truth only an indication of Paul's resolute *determination* to accomplish that very thing himself: to give one's own will the name of God, *thora*—that is essentially Jewish. Paul *wants* to dispose of the "wisdom of this world": his enemies are the *good* philologians and physicians of the Alexandrine school—on them he makes his war. As a matter of fact no man can be a *philologian* or a physician without being also *Antichrist*. That is to say, as a philologian a man sees *behind* the "holy books," and as a physician he sees *behind* the physiological degeneration of the typical Christian. The physician says "incurable"; the philologian says "fraud."...

48

—Has anyone ever clearly understood the celebrated story at the beginning of the Bible—of God's mortal terror of *science*?... No one, in fact, has understood it. This priest-book *par excellence* opens, as is fitting, with the great inner difficulty of the priest: *he* faces only one great danger; *ergo*, "God" faces only one great danger.—

The old God, wholly "spirit," wholly the high-priest, wholly perfect, is promenading his garden: he is bored and trying to kill time. Against boredom even gods struggle in vain.[1] What does he do? He creates man—man is entertaining... But then he notices that man is also bored. God's pity for the only form of distress that invades all paradises knows no bounds: so he forthwith creates other animals. God's first mistake: to man these other animals were not entertaining—he sought dominion over them;

1. A paraphrase of Schiller's "Against stupidity even gods struggle in vain."

he did not want to be an "animal" himself.—So God created woman. In the act he brought boredom to an end—and also many other things! Woman was the *second* mistake of God.—"Woman, at bottom, is a serpent, Heva"—every priest knows that; "from woman comes every evil in the world"—every priest knows that, too. *Ergo*, she is also to blame for *science*... It was through woman that man learned to taste of the tree of knowledge.—What happened? The old God was seized by mortal terror. Man himself had been his *greatest* blunder; he had created a rival to himself; science makes men *godlike*—it is all up with priests and gods when man becomes scientific!—*Moral*: science is the forbidden *per se*; it alone is forbidden. Science is the *first* of sins, the germ of all sins, the *original* sin. *This is all there is of morality.*—"Thou shall *not* know":—the rest follows from that.—God's mortal terror, however, did not hinder him from being shrewd. How is one to *protect* one's self against science? For a long while this was the capital problem. Answer: Out of paradise with man! Happiness, leisure, foster thought—and all thoughts are bad thoughts!—Man *must* not think.—And so the priest invents distress, death, the mortal dangers of childbirth, all sorts of misery, old age, decrepitude, above all, *sickness*—nothing but devices for making war on science! The troubles of man don't *allow* him to think... Nevertheless—how terrible!—, the edifice of knowledge begins to tower aloft, invading heaven, shadowing the gods—what is to be done?—The old God invents *war*; he separates the peoples; he makes men destroy one another (—the priests have always had need of war...). War—among other things, a great disturber of science!—Incredible! Knowledge, *deliverance from the priests*, prospers in spite of war.—So the old God comes to his final resolution: "Man has become scientific—*there is no help for it: he must be drowned!*"...

49

—I have been understood. At the opening of the Bible there is the *whole* psychology of the priest.—The priest knows of only one great danger: that is science—the sound comprehension of cause and effect. But science flourishes, on the whole, only under favourable conditions—a man must have time, he must have an *overflowing* intellect, in order to "know."... "*Therefore*, man must be made unhappy,"—this has been, in all ages, the logic of the priest.—It is easy to see just *what*, by this logic, was the first thing to come into the world:—"*sin*."... The concept of guilt and punishment, the whole "moral order of the world," was set up *against* science—*against* the deliverance of man from priests... Man must *not* look outward; he must look inward. He must *not* look at things shrewdly and cautiously, to learn about them; he must not look at all; he must *suffer*... And he must suffer so much that he is always in need of the priest.—Away with physicians! *What is needed is a Saviour.*—The concept of guilt and punishment, including the doctrines of "grace," of "salvation," of "forgiveness"—*lies* through and through, and absolutely without psychological reality—were devised to destroy man's *sense of causality*: they are an attack upon the concept of cause and effect!—And *not* an attack with the fist, with the knife, with honesty in hate and love! On the contrary, one inspired by the most cowardly, the most crafty, the most ignoble of instincts! An attack of *priests*! An attack of *parasites*! The vampirism of pale, subterranean leeches!... When the natural consequences of an act are no longer "natural," but are regarded as produced by the ghostly creations of superstition—by "God," by "spirits," by "souls"—and reckoned as merely "moral" consequences, as rewards, as punishments, as hints, as lessons, then the whole ground-work of knowledge is destroyed—*then the greatest of crimes against humanity has been perpetrated.*—I repeat that sin, man's self-desecration *par excellence*, was invented in order to make science, culture, and every elevation and ennobling of man impossible; the priest *rules* through the invention of sin.—

50

—In this place I can't permit myself to omit a psychology of "belief," of the "believer," for the special benefit of "believers." If there remain any today who do not yet know how *indecent* it is to be "believing"—*or* how much a sign of *décadence*, of a broken will to live—then they will know it well enough tomorrow. My voice reaches even the deaf.—It appears, unless I have been incorrectly informed, that there prevails among Christians a sort of criterion of truth that is called "proof by power." "Faith makes blessed: *therefore* it is true."—It might be objected right here that blessedness is not demonstrated, it is merely *promised*: it hangs upon "faith" as a condition—one *shall* be blessed *because* one believes... But what of the thing that the priest promises to the believer, the wholly transcendental "beyond"—how is *that* to be demonstrated?—The "proof by power," thus assumed, is actually no more at bottom than a belief that the effects which faith promises will not fail to appear. In a formula: "I believe that faith makes for blessedness—*therefore*, it is true."... But this is as far as we may go. This "therefore" would be *absurdum* itself as a criterion of truth.—But let us admit, for the sake of politeness, that blessedness by faith may be demonstrated (—*not* merely hoped for, and *not* merely promised by the suspicious lips of a priest):

even so, *could* blessedness—in a technical term, *pleasure*—ever be a proof of truth? So little is this true that it is almost a proof against truth when sensations of pleasure influence the answer to the question "What is true?" or, at all events, it is enough to make that "truth" highly suspicious. The proof by "pleasure" is a proof *of* "pleasure"—nothing more; why in the world should it be assumed that *true* judgments give more pleasure than false ones, and that, in conformity to some pre-established harmony, they necessarily bring agreeable feelings in their train?—The experience of all disciplined and profound minds teaches *the contrary*. Man has had to fight for every atom of the truth, and has had to pay for it almost everything that the heart, that human love, that human trust cling to. Greatness of soul is needed for this business: the service of truth is the hardest of all services.—What, then, is the meaning of *integrity* in things intellectual? It means that a man must be severe with his own heart, that he must scorn "beautiful feelings," and that he makes every Yea and Nay a matter of conscience!—Faith makes blessed: *therefore*, it lies...

51

The fact that faith, under certain circumstances, may work for blessedness, but that this blessedness produced by an *idée fixe* by no means makes the idea itself true, and the fact that faith actually moves no mountains, but instead *raises them up* where there were none before: all this is made sufficiently clear by a walk through a *lunatic asylum*. *Not*, of course, to a priest: for his instincts prompt him to the lie that sickness is not sickness and lunatic asylums not lunatic asylums. Christianity finds sickness *necessary*, just as the Greek spirit had need of a superabundance of health—the actual ulterior purpose of the whole system of salvation of the church is to *make* people ill. And the church itself—doesn't it set up a Catholic lunatic asylum as the ultimate ideal?—The whole earth as a madhouse?—The sort of religious man that the church *wants* is a typical *décadent*; the moment at which a religious crisis dominates a people is always marked by epidemics of nervous disorder; the "inner world" of the religious man is so much like the "inner world" of the over strung and exhausted that it is difficult to distinguish between them; the "highest" states of mind, held up before mankind by Christianity as of supreme worth, are actually epileptoid in form—the church has granted the name of holy only to lunatics or to gigantic frauds *in majorem dei honorem*... Once I ventured to designate the whole Christian system of *training*[1] in penance and salvation (now best studied in England) as a method of producing a *folie circulaire* upon a soil already prepared for it, which is to say, a soil thoroughly unhealthy. Not everyone may be a Christian: one is not "converted" to Christianity—one must first be sick enough for it... We others, who have the *courage* for health *and* likewise for contempt,—we may well despise a religion that teaches misunderstanding of the body! That refuses to rid itself of the superstition about the soul! That makes a "virtue" of insufficient nourishment! That combats health as a sort of enemy, devil, temptation! That persuades itself that it is possible to carry about a "perfect soul" in a cadaver of a body, and that, to this end, had to devise for itself a new concept of "perfection," a pale, sickly, idiotically ecstatic state of existence, so-called "holiness"—a holiness that is itself merely a series of symptoms of an impoverished, enervated and incurably disordered body!... The Christian movement,

1. The word *training* is in English in the text.

as a European movement, was from the start no more than a general uprising of all sorts of outcast and refuse elements (—who now, under cover of Christianity, aspire to power). It does *not* represent the decay of a race; it represents, on the contrary, a conglomeration of *décadence* products from all directions, crowding together and seeking one another out. It was *not*, as has been thought, the corruption of antiquity, of *noble* antiquity, which made Christianity possible; one cannot too sharply challenge the learned imbecility which today maintains that theory. At the time when the sick and rotten Chandala classes in the whole *imperium* were Christianized, the *contrary type*, the nobility, reached its finest and ripest development. The majority became master; democracy, with its Christian instincts, *triumphed...* Christianity was not "national," it was not based on race—it appealed to all the varieties of men disinherited by life, it had its allies everywhere. Christianity has the rancour of the sick at its very core—the instinct against the *healthy*, against *health*. Everything that is well-constituted, proud, gallant and, above all, beautiful gives offence to its ears and eyes. Again I remind you of Paul's priceless saying: "And God hath chosen the *weak* things of the world, the *foolish* things of the world, the *base* things of the world, and things which are *despised*":[1] *this* was the formula; *in hoc signo* the *décadence* triumphed.—*God on the cross*—is man always to miss the frightful inner significance of this symbol?—Everything that suffers, everything that hangs on the cross, is *divine...* We all hang on the cross, consequently *we* are divine... We alone are divine... Christianity was thus a victory: a nobler attitude of mind was destroyed by it—Christianity remains to this day the greatest misfortune of humanity.—

1. 1 Corinthians i, 27, 28.

52

Christianity also stands in opposition to all *intellectual* well-being,—sick reasoning is the only sort that it *can* use as Christian reasoning; it takes the side of everything that is idiotic; it pronounces a curse upon "intellect," upon the *superbia* of the healthy intellect. Since sickness is inherent in Christianity, it follows that the typically Christian state of "faith" *must* be a form of sickness too, and that all straight, straightforward and scientific paths to knowledge *must* be banned by the church as *forbidden* ways. Doubt is thus a sin from the start... The complete lack of psychological cleanliness in the priest—revealed by a glance at him—is a phenomenon *resulting* from *décadence*,—one may observe in hysterical women and in rachitic children how regularly the falsification of instincts, delight in lying for the mere sake of lying, and incapacity for looking straight and walking straight are symptoms of *décadence*. "Faith" means the will to avoid knowing what is true. The pietist, the priest of either sex, is a fraud *because* he is sick: his instinct *demands* that the truth shall never be allowed its rights on any point. "Whatever makes for illness is *good*; whatever issues from abundance, from superabundance, from power, is *evil*": so argues the believer. The *impulse to lie*—it is by this that I recognize every foreordained theologian.—Another characteristic of the theologian is his *unfitness for philology*. What I hear mean by philology is, in a general sense, the art of reading with profit—the capacity for absorbing facts *without* interpreting them falsely, and *without* losing caution, patience and subtlety in the effort to understand them. Philology as *ephexis*[1] in interpretation: whether one be dealing with books,

1. That is, to say, scepticism. Among the Greeks scepticism was also occasionally called ephecticism.

with newspaper reports, with the most fateful events or with weather statistics—not to mention the "salvation of the soul."... The way in which a theologian, whether in Berlin or in Rome, is ready to explain, say, a "passage of Scripture," or an experience, or a victory by the national army, by turning upon it the high illumination of the Psalms of David, is always so *daring* that it is enough to make a philologian run up a wall. But what shall he do when pietists and other such cows from Suabia[1] use the "finger of God" to convert their miserably commonplace and huggermugger existence into a miracle of "grace," a "providence" and an "experience of salvation"? The most modest exercise of the intellect, not to say of decency, should certainly be enough to convince these interpreters of the perfect childishness and unworthiness of such a misuse of the divine digital dexterity. However small our piety, if we ever encountered a god who always cured us of a cold in the head at just the right time, or got us into our carriage at the very instant heavy rain began to fall, he would seem so absurd a god that he'd have to be abolished even if he existed. God as a domestic servant, as a letter carrier, as an almanac-man—at bottom, he is a mere name for the stupidest sort of chance... "Divine Providence," which every third man in "educated Germany" still believes in, is so strong an argument against God that it would be impossible to think of a stronger. And in any case it is an argument against Germans!...

1. A reference to the University of Tübingen and its famous school of Biblical criticism. The leader of this school was F. C. Baur, and one of the men greatly influenced by it was Nietzsche's pet abomination, David F. Strauss, himself a Suabian. *Vide* § 10 and § 28.

53

—It is so little true that *martyrs* offer any support to the truth of a cause that I am inclined to deny that any martyr has ever had anything to do with the truth at all. In the very tone in which a martyr flings what he fancies to be true at the head of the world there appears so low a grade of intellectual honesty and such *insensibility* to the problem of "truth," that it is never necessary to refute him. Truth is not something that one man has and another man has not: at best, only peasants, or peasant-apostles like Luther, can think of truth in any such way. One may rest assured that the greater the degree of a man's intellectual conscience the greater will be his modesty, his *discretion*, on this point. To *know* in five cases, and to refuse, with delicacy, to know anything *further*... "Truth," as the word is understood by every prophet, every sectarian, every free-thinker, every Socialist and every churchman, is simply a complete proof that not even a beginning has been made in the intellectual discipline and self-control that are necessary to the unearthing of even the smallest truth.—The deaths of the martyrs, it may be said in passing, have been misfortunes of history: they have *misled*... The conclusion that all idiots, women and plebeians come to, that there must be something in a cause for which any one goes to his death (or which, as under primitive Christianity, sets off epidemics of death-seeking)—this conclusion has been an unspeakable drag upon the testing of facts, upon the whole spirit of inquiry and investigation. The martyrs have *damaged* the truth... Even to this day the crude fact of persecution is enough to give an honourable name to the most empty sort of sectarianism.—But why? Is the worth of a cause altered by the fact that someone had laid down his life for it?—An error that becomes honourable is simply an error that has acquired one seductive charm the more: do you suppose, Messrs. Theologians, that we shall give you the chance to be martyred for your lies?—One best disposes of a cause by respectfully putting it on ice—that is also the best way to dispose of theologians... This was precisely the world- historical stupidity of all the persecutors: that they gave the appearance of honour to the cause they opposed—that they made it a present of the fascination of martyrdom... Women are still on their knees before an error because they have been told that someone died on the cross for it. *Is the cross, then, an argument?*—But about all these things there is one, and one only, who has said what has been needed for thousands of years—*Zarathustra*.

They made signs in blood along the way that they went, and their folly taught them that the truth is proved by blood.

But blood is the worst of all testimonies to the truth; blood poisoneth even the purest teaching and turneth it into madness and hatred in the heart.

And when one goeth through fire for his teaching—what doth that prove? Verily, it is more when one's teaching cometh out of one's own burning![1]

54

Do not let yourself be deceived: great intellects are sceptical. Zarathustra is a sceptic. The strength, the *freedom* which proceed from intellectual power, from a superabundance of intellectual power, *manifest* themselves as scepticism. Men of fixed convictions do not count when it comes to determining what is funda-

1. The quotations are from "Also sprach Zarathustra" ii, 24: "Of Priests."

mental in values and lack of values. Men of convictions are prisoners. They do not see far enough, they do not see what is *below* them: whereas a man who would talk to any purpose about value and non-value must be able to see five hundred convictions *beneath* him—and *behind* him... A mind that aspires to great things, and that wills the means thereto, is necessarily sceptical. Freedom from any sort of conviction *belongs* to strength, and to an independent point of view... That grand passion which is at once the foundation and the power of a sceptic's existence, and is both more enlightened and more despotic than he is himself, drafts the whole of his intellect into its service; it makes him unscrupulous; it gives him courage to employ unholy means; under certain circumstances it does not *begrudge* him even convictions. Conviction as a means: one may achieve a good deal by means of a conviction. A grand passion makes use of and uses up convictions; it does not yield to them—it knows itself to be sovereign.—On the contrary, the need of faith, of something unconditioned by yea or nay, of Carlylism, if I may be allowed the word, is a need of *weakness*. The man of faith, the "believer" of any sort, is necessarily a dependent man—such a man cannot posit *himself* as a goal, nor can he find goals within himself. The "believer" does not belong to himself; he can only be a means to an end; he must be *used up*; he needs someone to use him up. His instinct gives the highest honours to an ethic of self-effacement; he is prompted to embrace it by everything: his prudence, his experience, his vanity. Every sort of faith is in itself an evidence of self-effacement, of self-estrangement... When one reflects how necessary it is to the great majority that there be regulations to restrain them from without and hold them fast, and to what extent control, or, in a higher sense, *slavery*, is the one and only condition which makes for the well-being of the weak-willed man, and especially woman, then one at once understands conviction and "faith." To the man with convictions they are his backbone. To *avoid* seeing many things, to be impartial about nothing, to be a party man through and through, to estimate all values strictly and infallibly—these are conditions necessary to the existence of such a man. But by the same token they are *antagonists* of the truthful man—of the truth... The believer is not free to answer the question, "true" or "not true," according to the dictates of his own conscience: integrity on *this* point would work his instant downfall. The pathological limitations of his vision turn the man of convictions into a fanatic—Savonarola, Luther, Rousseau, Robespierre, Saint-Simon—these types stand in opposition to the strong, *emancipated* spirit. But the grandiose attitudes of these *sick* intellects, these intellectual epileptics, are of influence upon the great masses—fanatics are picturesque, and mankind prefers observing poses to listening to *reasons*...

55

—One step further in the psychology of conviction, of "faith." It is now a good while since I first proposed for consideration the question whether convictions are not even more dangerous enemies to truth than lies. ("Human, All-Too-Human," I, aphorism 483.)[1] This time I desire to put the question definitely: is there any actual difference between a lie and a conviction?— All the world believes that there is; but what is not believed by all the world!—Every conviction has its history, its primitive forms, its stage of tentativeness and error: it *becomes* a conviction only after

1. The aphorism, which is headed "The Enemies of Truth," makes the direct statement: "Convictions are more dangerous enemies of truth than lies."

having been, for a long time, *not* one, and then, for an even longer time, *hardly* one. What if falsehood be also one of these embryonic forms of conviction?—Sometimes all that is needed is a change in persons: what was a lie in the father becomes a conviction in the son.—I call it lying to refuse to see what one sees, or to refuse to see it *as* it is: whether the lie be uttered before witnesses or not before witnesses is of no consequence. The most common sort of lie is that by which a man deceives himself: the deception of others is a relatively rare offence.—Now, this will *not* to see what one sees, this will *not* to see it as it is, is almost the first requisite for all who belong to a party of whatever sort: the party man becomes inevitably a liar. For example, the German historians are convinced that Rome was synonymous with despotism and that the Germanic peoples brought the spirit of liberty into the world: what is the difference between this conviction and a lie? Is it to be wondered at that all partisans, including the German historians, instinctively roll the fine phrases of morality upon their tongues—that morality almost owes its very *survival* to the fact that the party man of every sort has need of it every moment?—"This is *our* conviction: we publish it to the whole world; we live and die for it—let us respect all who have convictions!"—I have actually heard such sentiments from the mouths of anti-Semites. On the contrary, gentlemen! An anti-Semite surely does not become more respectable because he lies on principle... The priests, who have more finesse in such matters, and who well understand the objection that lies against the notion of a conviction, which is to say, of a falsehood that becomes a matter of principle *because* it serves a purpose, have borrowed from the Jews the shrewd device of sneaking in the concepts, "God," "the will of God" and "the revelation of God" at this place. Kant, too, with his categorical imperative, was on the same road: this was his *practical* reason.[1] There are questions regarding the truth or untruth of which it is *not* for man to decide; all the capital questions, all the capital problems of valuation, are beyond human reason... To know the limits of reason—*that* alone is genuine philosophy... Why did God make a revelation to man? Would God have done anything superfluous? Man *could* not find out for himself what was good and what was evil, so God taught him His will... Moral: the priest does *not* lie—the question, "true" or "untrue," has nothing to do with such things as the priest discusses; it is impossible to lie about these things. In order to lie here it would be necessary to know *what* is true. But this is more than man *can* know; therefore, the priest is simply the mouthpiece of God.—Such a priestly syllogism is by no means merely Jewish and Christian; the right to lie and the *shrewd dodge* of "revelation" belong to the general priestly type—to the priest of the *décadence* as well as to the priest of pagan times (—Pagans are all those who say yes to life, and to whom "God" is a word signifying acquiescence in all things).—The "law," the "will of God," the "holy book," and "inspiration"—all these things are merely words for the conditions *under* which the priest comes to power and *with* which he maintains his power,—these concepts are to be found at the bottom of all priestly organizations, and of all priestly or priestly-philosophical schemes of governments. The "holy lie"—common alike to Confucius, to the Code of Manu, to Mohammed and to the Christian church—is not even wanting in Plato. "Truth is here": this means, no matter where it is heard, *the priest lies*...

1. A reference, of course, to Kant's "Kritik der praktischen Vernunft" (Critique of Practical Reason).

56

—In the last analysis it comes to this: what is the *end* of lying? The fact that, in Christianity, "holy" ends are not visible is *my* objection to the means it employs. Only *bad* ends appear: the poisoning, the calumniation, the denial of life, the despising of the body, the degradation and self-contamination of man by the concept of sin—*therefore*, its means are also bad.—I have a contrary feeling when I read the Code of Manu, an incomparably more intellectual and superior work, which it would be a sin against the *intelligence* to so much as *name* in the same breath with the Bible. It is easy to see why: there is a genuine philosophy behind it, *in* it, not merely an evil-smelling mess of Jewish rabbinism and superstition,—it gives even the most fastidious psychologist something to sink his teeth into. And, *not* to forget what is most important, it differs fundamentally from every kind of Bible: by means of it the *nobles*, the philosophers and the warriors keep the whip-hand over the majority; it is full of noble valuations, it shows a feeling of perfection, an acceptance of life, and triumphant feeling toward self and life—the *sun* shines upon the whole book.—All the things on which Christianity vents its fathomless vulgarity—for example, procreation, women and marriage—are here handled earnestly, with reverence and with love and confidence. How can anyone really put into the hands of children and ladies a book which contains such vile things as this: "to avoid fornication, let every man have his own wife, and let every woman have her own husband;... it is better to marry than to burn"?[1] And is it *possible* to be a Christian so long as the origin of man is Christianized, which is to say, *befouled*, by

1. 1 Corinthians vii, 2, 9.

the doctrine of the *immaculata conceptio*?... I know of no book in which so many delicate and kindly things are said of women as in the Code of Manu; these old grey-beards and saints have a way of being gallant to women that it would be impossible, perhaps, to surpass. "The mouth of a woman," it says in one place, "the breasts of a maiden, the prayer of a child and the smoke of sacrifice are always pure." In another place: "there is nothing purer than the light of the sun, the shadow cast by a cow, air, water, fire and the breath of a maiden." Finally, in still another place—perhaps this is also a holy lie—: "all the orifices of the body above the navel are pure, and all below are impure. Only in the maiden is the whole body pure."

57

One catches the *unholiness* of Christian means *in flagranti* by the simple process of putting the ends sought by Christianity beside the ends sought by the Code of Manu—by putting these enormously antithetical ends under a strong light. The critic of Christianity cannot evade the necessity of making Christianity *contemptible*.—A book of laws such as the Code of Manu has the same origin as every other good law-book: it epitomizes the experience, the sagacity and the ethical experimentation of long centuries; it brings things to a conclusion; it no longer creates. The prerequisite to a codification of this sort is recognition of the fact that the means which establish the authority of a slowly and painfully attained *truth* are fundamentally different from those which one would make use of to prove it. A law-book never recites the utility, the grounds, the casuistical antecedents of a law: for if it did so it would lose the imperative tone, the "thou shall," on which obedience is based. The problem lies exactly here.—At a certain point in the evolution of a people, the class within it of the greatest insight, which is to say, the greatest hindsight and foresight, declares that the series of experiences determining how all shall live—or *can* live—has come to an end. The object now is to reap as rich and as complete a harvest as possible from the days of experiment and *hard* experience. In consequence, the thing that is to be avoided above everything is further experimentation—the continuation of the state in which values are fluent, and are tested, chosen and criticized *ad infinitum.* Against this a double wall is set up: on the one hand, *revelation*, which is the assumption that the reasons lying behind the laws are *not* of human origin, that they were *not* sought out and found by a slow process and after many errors, but that they are of divine ancestry, and came into being complete, perfect, without a history, as a free gift, a miracle...; and on the other hand, *tradition*, which is the assumption that the law has stood unchanged from time immemorial, and that it is impious and a crime against one's forefathers to bring it into question. The authority of the law is thus grounded on the thesis: God gave it, and the fathers *lived* it.—The higher motive of such procedure lies in the design to distract consciousness, step by step, from its concern with notions of right living (that is to say, those that have been *proved* to be right by wide and carefully considered experience), so that instinct attains to a perfect automatism—a primary necessity to every sort of mastery, to every sort of perfection in the art of life. To draw up such a law-book as Manu's means to lay before a people the possibility of future mastery, of attainable perfection—it permits them to aspire to the highest reaches of the art of life. *To that end the thing must be made unconscious*: that is the aim of every holy lie.—The *order of castes*, the highest, the dominating law, is merely the ratification of an *order of nature*, of a natural law of the first rank, over which no arbitrary fiat, no "modern idea," can exert any influence. In every healthy society there are three physiological types, gravitating toward differentiation but mutually conditioning one another, and each of these has its own hygiene, its own sphere of work, its own special mastery and feeling of perfection. It is *not* Manu but nature that sets off in one class those who are chiefly intellectual, in another those who are marked by muscular strength and temperament, and in a third those who are distinguished in neither one way or the other, but show only mediocrity—the last-named represents the great majority, and the first two the select. The superior caste—I call it the *fewest*—has, as the most perfect, the privileges of the few: it stands for happiness, for beauty, for everything good upon earth. Only the most intellectual of men have any right to beauty, to the beautiful; only in them can goodness escape being weakness. *Pulchrum est paucorum hominum*:[1] goodness is a privilege. Nothing could be more unbecoming to them than uncouth manners or a pessimistic look, or an eye that sees *ugliness*—or indignation against the general aspect of things. Indignation is the privilege of the Chandala; so is pessimism. "*The world is perfect*"—so prompts the instinct of the intellectual, the instinct of the man who says yes to life. "Imperfection, whatever is *inferior* to us, distance, the pathos of distance, even the Chandala themselves are parts of this perfection." The most intelligent men, like the *strongest*, find their happiness where others would find only disaster: in the labyrinth, in being hard with themselves and with others, in effort; their delight is in self-mastery; in them asceticism becomes second nature, a necessity,

1. Few men are noble.

an instinct. They regard a difficult task as a privilege; it is to them a *recreation* to play with burdens that would crush all others... Knowledge—a form of asceticism.—They are the most honourable kind of men: but that does not prevent them being the most cheerful and most amiable. They rule, not because they want to, but because they *are*; they are not at liberty to play second.—The *second caste*: to this belong the guardians of the law, the keepers of order and security, the more noble warriors, above all, the king as the highest form of warrior, judge and preserver of the law. The second in rank constitute the executive arm of the intellectuals, the next to them in rank, taking from them all that is *rough* in the business of ruling—their followers, their right hand, their most apt disciples.—In all this, I repeat, there is nothing arbitrary, nothing "made up"; whatever is to the *contrary* is made up—by its nature is brought to shame... The order of castes, the *order of rank*, simply formulates the supreme law of life itself; the separation of the three types is necessary to the maintenance of society, and to the evolution of higher types, and the highest types—the *inequality* of rights is essential to the existence of any rights at all.—A right is a privilege. Everyone enjoys the privileges that accord with his state of existence. Let us not underestimate the privileges of the *mediocre*. Life is always harder as one mounts the *heights*—the cold increases, responsibility increases. A high civilization is a pyramid: it can stand only on a broad base; its primary prerequisite is a strong and soundly consolidated mediocrity. The handicrafts, commerce, agriculture, *science*, the greater part of art, in brief, the whole range of *occupational* activities, are compatible only with mediocre ability and aspiration; such callings would be out of place for exceptional men; the instincts which belong to them stand as much opposed to aristocracy as to anarchism. The fact that a man is publicly useful, that he is a wheel, a function, is evidence of a natural predisposition; it is not *society*, but the only sort of happiness that the majority are capable of, that makes them intelligent machines. To the mediocre mediocrity is a form of happiness; they have a natural instinct for mastering one thing, for specialization. It would be altogether unworthy of a profound intellect to see anything objectionable in mediocrity in itself. It is, in fact, the *first* prerequisite to the appearance of the exceptional: it is a necessary condition to a high degree of civilization. When the exceptional man handles the mediocre man with more delicate fingers than he applies to himself or to his equals, this is not merely kindness of heart—it is simply his *duty*... Whom do I hate most heartily among the rabbles of today? The rabble of Socialists, the apostles to the Chandala, who undermine the workingman's instincts, his pleasure, his feeling of contentment with his petty existence — who make him envious and teach him revenge... Wrong never lies in unequal rights; it lies in the assertion of "equal" rights... What is *bad*? But I have already answered: all that proceeds from weakness, from envy, from *revenge*.—The anarchist and the Christian have the same ancestry...

58

In point of fact, the end for which one lies makes a great difference: whether one preserves thereby or destroys. There is a perfect likeness between Christian and anarchist: their object, their instinct, points only toward destruction. One need only turn to history for a proof of this: there it appears with appalling distinctness. We have just studied a code of religious legislation whose object it was to convert the conditions which cause life to *flourish* into an "eternal" social organization,—Christianity found its mission in putting an end to such an organization, *because life flourished under it.* There the benefits that reason had produced during long ages of experiment and insecurity were applied to the most remote uses, and an effort was made to bring in a harvest that should be as large, as rich and as complete as possible; here, on the contrary, the harvest is *blighted* overnight... That which stood there *aere perennis*, the *imperium Romanum*, the most magnificent form of organization under difficult conditions that has ever been achieved, and compared to which everything before it and after it appears as patchwork, bungling, *dilletantism*—those holy anarchists made it a matter of "piety" to destroy "the world," *which is to say*, the *imperium Romanum*, so that in the end not a stone stood upon another—and even Germans and other such louts were able to become its masters... The Christian and the anarchist: both are *décadents*; both are incapable of any act that is not disintegrating, poisonous, degenerating, *blood-sucking*; both have an instinct of *mortal hatred* of everything that stands up, and is great, and has durability, and promises life a future... Christianity was the vampire of the *imperium Romanum*,—overnight it destroyed the vast achievement of the Romans: the conquest of the soil for a great culture *that could await its time*. Can it be that this fact is not yet understood? The *imperium Romanum* that we know, and that the history of the Roman provinces teaches us to know better and better,—this most admirable of all works of art in the grand manner was merely the beginning, and the structure to follow was not to *prove* its worth for thousands of years. To this day, nothing on a like scale *sub specie aeterni* has been brought into being, or even dreamed of!—This organization was strong enough to withstand bad emperors: the accident of personality has nothing to do with such things—the *first* principle of all genuinely great architecture. But it was not strong enough to stand up against the *corruptest* of all forms of corruption—against Christians... These stealthy worms, which under the cover of night, mist and duplicity, crept upon every individual, sucking him dry of all earnest interest in *real* things, of all instinct for *reality*—this cowardly, effeminate and sugar-coated gang gradually alienated all "souls," step by step, from that colossal edifice, turning against it all the meritorious, manly and noble natures that had found in the cause of Rome their own cause, their own serious purpose, their own *pride*. The sneakishness of hypocrisy, the secrecy of the conventicle, concepts as black as hell, such as the sacrifice of the innocent, the *union mystica* in the drinking of blood, above all, the slowly rekindled fire of revenge, of Chandala revenge—all *that* sort of thing became master of Rome: the same kind of religion which, in a pre-existent form, Epicurus had combatted. One has but to read Lucretius to know *what* Epicurus made war upon—*not* paganism, but "Christianity," which is to say, the corruption of souls by means of the concepts of guilt, punishment and immortality.—He combatted the *subterranean* cults, the whole of latent Christianity—to deny immortality was already a form of genuine *salvation*.—Epicurus had triumphed, and every respectable intellect in Rome was Epicurean—*when Paul appeared*... Paul, the Chandala hatred of Rome, of "the world," in the flesh and inspired by genius—the Jew, the *eternal* Jew *par excellence*... What he saw was how, with the aid of the small sectarian Christian movement that stood apart from Judaism, a "world conflagration" might be kindled; how, with the symbol of "God on the cross," all secret seditions, all the fruits of anarchistic intrigues in the empire, might be amalgamated into one immense power. "Salvation is of the Jews."—Christianity is the formula for exceeding *and* summing up the subterranean cults of all varieties, that of Osiris, that of the Great Mother, that of Mithras, for instance: in his discernment of this fact the genius of Paul showed itself. His instinct was here so sure that, with reckless violence to the truth, he put the ideas which lent fascination to every sort of Chandala religion into the mouth of the "Saviour" as his own inventions, and not only into the mouth—he *made* out of him something that even a priest of Mithras could understand... This was his revelation at Damascus: he grasped the fact that he *needed* the belief in immortality in order to rob "the world" of its value, that the concept of "hell" would master Rome—that the notion of a "beyond" is the *death of life*... Nihilist and Christian: they rhyme in German, and they do more than rhyme...

59

The whole labour of the ancient world gone for *naught*: I have no word to describe the feelings that such an enormity arouses in me.—And, considering the fact that its labour was merely preparatory, that with adamantine self-consciousness it laid only the foundations for a work to go on for thousands of years, the whole *meaning* of antiquity disappears!... To what end the Greeks? to what end the Romans?—All the prerequisites to a learned culture, all the *methods* of science, were already there; man had already perfected the great and incomparable art of reading profitably—that first necessity to the tradition of culture, the unity of the sciences; the natural sciences, in alliance with mathematics and mechanics, were on the right road,—*the sense of fact*, the last and more valuable of all the senses, had its schools, and its traditions were already centuries old! Is all this properly understood?

Every *essential* to the beginning of the work was ready:—and the *most* essential, it cannot be said too often, are methods, and also the most difficult to develop, and the longest opposed by habit and laziness. What we have today reconquered, with unspeakable self-discipline, for ourselves—for certain bad instincts, certain Christian instincts, still lurk in our bodies—that is to say, the keen eye for reality, the cautious hand, patience and seriousness in the smallest things, the whole *integrity* of knowledge—all these things were already there, and had been there for two thousand years! *More*, there was also a refined and excellent tact and taste! *Not* as mere brain-drilling! *Not* as "German" culture, with its loutish manners! But as body, as bearing, as instinct—in short, as reality... *All gone for naught!* Overnight it became merely a memory!—The Greeks! The Romans! Instinctive nobility, taste, methodical inquiry, genius for organization and administration, faith in and the *will* to secure the future of man, a great yes to everything entering into the *imperium Romanum* and palpable to all the senses, a grand style that was beyond mere art, but had become reality, truth, *life*...—All overwhelmed in a night, but not by a convulsion of nature! Not trampled to death by Teutons and others of heavy hoof! But brought to shame by crafty, sneaking, invisible, anæmic vampires! Not conquered,—only sucked dry!... Hidden vengefulness, petty envy, became *master*! Everything wretched, intrinsically ailing, and invaded by bad feelings, the whole *ghetto-world* of the soul, was at once *on top*!—One needs but read any of the Christian agitators, for example, St. Augustine, in order to realize, in order to smell, what filthy fellows came to the top. It would be an error, however, to assume that there was any lack of understanding in the leaders of the Christian movement:—ah, but they were clever, clever to the point of holiness, these fathers of the church! What they lacked was something quite different. Nature neglected—perhaps forgot—to give them even the most modest endowment of respectable, of upright, of *cleanly* instincts... Between ourselves, they are not even men... If Islam despises Christianity, it has a thousand fold right to do so: Islam at least assumes that it is dealing with *men*...

60

Christianity destroyed for us the whole harvest of ancient civilization, and later it also destroyed for us the whole harvest of *Mohammedan* civilization. The wonderful culture of the Moors in Spain, which was fundamentally nearer to *us* and appealed more to our senses and tastes than that of Rome and Greece, was *trampled down* (—I do not say by what sort of feet—) Why? Because it had to thank noble and manly instincts for its origin—because it said yes to life, even to the rare and refined luxuriousness of Moorish life!... The crusaders later made war on something before which it would have been more fitting for them to have grovelled in the dust—a civilization beside which even that of our nineteenth century seems very poor and very "senile."—What they wanted, of course, was booty: the orient was rich... Let us put aside our prejudices! The crusades were a higher form of piracy, nothing more! The German nobility, which is fundamentally a Viking nobility, was in its element there: the church knew only too well how the German nobility was to be *won*... The German noble, always the "Swiss guard" of the church, always in the service of every bad instinct of the church—*but well paid*... Consider the fact that it is precisely the aid of German swords and German blood and valour that has enabled the church to carry through its war to the death upon everything noble on earth! At this point a host of painful questions suggest themselves. The German nobility stands *outside* the history of the higher civilization: the reason is obvious... Christianity, alcohol—the two *great* means of corruption... Intrinsically there should be no more choice between Islam and Christianity than there is between an Arab and a Jew. The decision is already reached; nobody remains at liberty to choose here. Either a man is a Chandala or he is not... "War to the knife with Rome! Peace and friendship with Islam!": this was the feeling, this was the *act*, of that great free spirit, that genius among German emperors, Frederick II. What! Must a German first be a genius, a free spirit, before he can feel *decently*? I can't make out how a German could ever feel *Christian*...

61

Here it becomes necessary to call up a memory that must be a hundred times more painful to Germans. The Germans have destroyed for Europe the last great harvest of civilization that Europe was ever to reap—the *Renaissance*. Is it understood at last, *will* it ever be understood, *what* the Renaissance was? *The transvaluation of Christian values*,—an attempt with all available means, all instincts and all the resources of genius to bring about a triumph of the *opposite* values, the more *noble* values... This has been the one great war of the past; there has never been a more critical question than that of the Renaissance—it is *my* question too—; there has never been a form of *attack* more fundamental, more direct, or more violently delivered by a whole front upon the center of the enemy! To attack at the critical place, at the very seat of Christianity, and there enthrone the more noble values—

that is to say, to *insinuate* them into the instincts, into the most fundamental needs and appetites of those sitting there... I see before me the *possibility* of a perfectly heavenly enchantment and spectacle:—it seems to me to scintillate with all the vibrations of a fine and delicate beauty, and within it there is an art so divine, so infernally divine, that one might search in vain for thousands of years for another such possibility; I see a spectacle so rich in significance and at the same time so wonderfully full of paradox that it should arouse all the gods on Olympus to immortal laughter—*Cæsar Borgia as pope!*... Am I understood?... Well then, *that* would have been the sort of triumph that *I* alone am longing for today—: by it Christianity would have been *swept away*!—What happened? A German monk, Luther, came to Rome. This monk, with all the vengeful instincts of an unsuccessful priest in him, raised a rebellion *against* the Renaissance in Rome... Instead of grasping, with profound thanksgiving, the miracle that had taken place: the conquest of Christianity at its *capital*—instead of this, his hatred was stimulated by the spectacle. A religious man thinks only of himself.—Luther saw only the *depravity* of the papacy at the very moment when the oppo site was becoming apparent: the old corruption, the *peccatum originale*, Christianity itself, no longer occupied the papal chair! Instead there was life! Instead there was the triumph of life! Instead there was a great yea to all lofty, beautiful and daring things!... And Luther *restored the church*: he attacked it... The Renaissance—an event without meaning, a great futility!—Ah, these Germans, what they have not cost us! *Futility*—that has always been the work of the Germans.—The Reformation; Leibnitz; Kant and so-called German philosophy; the war of "liberation"; the empire—every time a futile substitute for something that once existed, for something *irrecoverable*... These Germans, I confess, are my enemies:

I despise all their un-cleanliness in concept and valuation, their cowardice before every honest yea and nay. For nearly a thousand years they have tangled and confused everything their fingers have touched; they have on their conscience all the half-way measures, all the three-eighths-way measures, that Europe is sick of,—they also have on their conscience the un-cleanest variety of Christianity that exists, and the most incurable and indestructible—Protestantism... If mankind never manages to get rid of Christianity the *Germans* will be to blame...

62

—With this I come to a conclusion and pronounce my judgment. I condemn Christianity; I bring against the Christian church the most terrible of all the accusations that an accuser has ever had in his mouth. It is, to me, the greatest of all imaginable corruptions; it seeks to work the ultimate corruption, the worst possible corruption. The Christian church has left nothing untouched by its depravity; it has turned every value into worthlessness, and every truth into a lie, and every integrity into baseness of soul. Let anyone dare to speak to me of its "humanitarian" blessings! Its deepest necessities range it against any effort to abolish distress; it lives by distress; it creates distress to make itself immortal... For example, the worm of sin: it was the church that first enriched mankind with this misery!- The "equality of souls before God"—this fraud, this pretext for the rancunes of all the base-minded—this explosive concept, ending in revolution, the modern idea, and the notion of overthrowing the whole social order—this is Christian dynamite... The "humanitarian" blessings of Christianity forsooth! To breed out of humanitas a self-contradiction, an art of self-pollution, a will to lie at any price, an aversion and contempt for all good and honest instincts! All this, to me, is the "humanitarianism" of Christianity!—Parasitism as the only practice of the church; with its anæmic and "holy" ideals, sucking all the blood, all the love, all the hope out of life; the beyond as the will to deny all reality; the cross as the distinguishing mark of the most subterranean conspiracy ever heard of,—against health, beauty, well-being, intellect, kindness of soul—against life itself...

INTERNATIONAL BESTSELLER

The Knowledge of the Holy

by A.W. Tozer

Pages	:	136
Size	:	8x5.25 inches
Binding	:	Paperback
Language	:	English
Subject	:	Mind, Body & Spirit
ISBN	:	9789389157130

'The Knowledge of the Holy' by A.W. Tozer illuminates God's attributes—from wisdom, to grace, to merchant in doing so, attempts to restore the majesty and wonder of God in the hearts and minds of all Christians. It teaches us how we can rejuvenate our prayer life, meditate more Reverently, understand God more deeply and experience God's presence in our daily lives.

OTHER BOOKS YOU MAY LIKE

- 1984 by George Orwell, ISBN: 9789380914947
- 12 Years a Slave by Solomon Northup, ISBN: 9789390492374
- 51 Most Powerful Prayers by Ryan, ISBN: 9789354990847
- A Christmas Carol by Charles Dickens, ISBN: 9788193545874
- A Cloud by Day, a Fire by Night by AW Tozer, ISBN: 9789354990854
- A Passage to India by E.M. Forster, ISBN: 9789354990205
- A Room of One's Own by Virginia Woolf, ISBN: 9789354990281
- A Streetcar Named Desire by Tennessee Williams, ISBN: 9788194748601
- A Wrinkle in Time by Madeleine L'Engle, ISBN: 9789354991066
- Abraham Lincoln by Lord Charnwood, ISBN: 9789380914251
- Absolute Surrender by Andrew Murray, ISBN: 9789389716269
- Animal Farm by George Orwell, ISBN: 9789380914701
- Anthem by Ayn Rand, ISBN: 9789389157079
- As a Man Thinketh by James Allen, ISBN: 9788180320262
- As I Lay Dying by William Faulkner, ISBN: 9789390492381
- Awakened Imagination by Neville Goddard, ISBN: 9789389157086
- Be What You Wish by Neville Goddard, ISBN: 9789387669550
- Chanakya Neeti by Chanakya, ISBN: 9789389716276
- Civilization and Its Discontents by Sigmund Freud, ISBN: 9789387669499
- Delighting in God by AW Tozer, ISBN: 9788194748632
- Demian by Hermann Hesse, ISBN: 9789387669567
- Experiencing the Holy Spirit by Andrew Murray, ISBN: 9788194764809
- Feeling is the Secret by Neville Goddard, ISBN: 9789389157109
- George Orwell Combo : Animal Farm & 1984, ISBN: 9789390492459
- Gravity by George Gamow, ISBN: 9789388118484
- Guerrilla Warfare by Ernesto Che Guevara, ISBN: 9789354990366

Develop your reading habit | **Gift books to your friends**

OTHER BOOKS YOU MAY LIKE

- How to be filled with the Holy Spirit by AW Tozer, ISBN: 9789389157116
- How to Develop Self Confidence by Dale Carnegie, ISBN: 9789387669000
- In His Steps by Charles M. Sheldon, ISBN: 9789390492794
- Life of Christ by Fulton J. Sheen, ISBN: 9789389716306
- Lost Horizon by James Hilton, ISBN: 9789389716313
- Man: The Dwelling Place of God by AW Tozer, ISBN: 9789354990656
- Maneaters of Kumaon by Jim Corbett, ISBN: 9789354990731
- Mansarover 1 (Hindi) by Premchand, ISBN: 9789380914978
- Mansarover 2 (Hindi) by Premchand, ISBN: 9789380914985
- Meditation and Its Methods by Swami Vivekananda, ISBN: 9789389716320
- One, None and a Hundred Thousand by Luigi Pirandello, ISBN: 9789389716337
- Paths to Power by AW Tozer, ISBN: Forthcoming
- Scientific Healing Affirmations by P. Yogananda, ISBN: 9789389716344
- Selected Stories of Rabindranath Tagore by Tagore, ISBN: 9789380914770
- Siddhartha by Hermann Hesse, ISBN: 9789380914145
- Student's Encyclopedia of G. K. by GP Editors, ISBN: 9789380914190
- Tales from Shakespeare by Charles Lamb & Mary Lamb, ISBN: 9789380914367
- The Alchemy of Happiness by Al-Ghazzali, ISBN: 9789387669505
- The Book of Enoch by Enoch, ISBN: 9789390492480
- The Dynamic Laws of Prosperity by Catherine Ponder, ISBN: 9789388118156
- The Game of Life and How to Play It by Florence Shinn, ISBN: 9789387669390
- The Imitation of Christ by Thomas A Kempis, ISBN: 9789388118057
- The Knowledge of the Holy by AW Tozer, ISBN: 9789389157130
- The Law by Neville Goddard, ISBN: 9789390492886
- The Light of Asia by Sir Edwin Arnold, ISBN: 9789380914923
- The Magic of Believing by Claudie Bristol, ISBN: 9789388118149

Develop your reading habit | **Gift books to your friends**

OTHER BOOKS YOU MAY LIKE

- The Magic of Faith by Joseph Murphy, ISBN: 9789388118743
- The Miracles of Your Mind by Joseph Murphy, ISBN: 9788180320743
- The Mysterious Affair at Styles by Agatha Christie, ISBN: 9789390492510
- The Origin of Species by Charles Darwin, ISBN: 9788180320453
- The Plague by Albert Camus, ISBN: 9788194764892
- The Power of Awareness by Neville Goddard, ISBN: 9789387669406
- The Power of Positive Thinking by Norman Vincent Peale, ISBN: 9789388118569
- The Problem of Increasing Human Energy by Nikola Tesla, ISBN: 9789354990953
- The Prophet by Kahlil Gibran, ISBN: 9789380914022
- The Psychopathology of Everyday Life by Sigmund Freud, ISBN: 9789388118071
- The Pursuit of God by AW Tozer, ISBN: 9789389157147
- The Railway Children by E Nesbit, ISBN: 9789354990960
- The Red Badge of Courage by Stephen Crane, ISBN: 9789354990977
- The Sound and the Fury by William Faulkner, ISBN: 9789390492572
- The Stranger by Albert Camus, ISBN: 9789390492589
- The Sun Also Rises by Ernest Hemingway, ISBN: 9789354990984
- The Yoga Sutras of Patanjali by Patanjali, ISBN: 9789389716351
- Their Eyes Were Watching God by Zora Neale Hurston, ISBN: 9788194764885
- Think and Grow Rich by Napoleon Hill, ISBN: 9788180320255
- Thought Vibration by William Walker Atkinson, ISBN: 9789389157154
- To the Lighthouse by Virginia Woolf, ISBN: 9789390492190
- Who were the Shudras by Dr B.R. Ambedkar, ISBN: 9789354991028
- World's Best Short Stories: Volume 1 by Various Authors, ISBN: 9789390492275
- Wuthering Heights by Emily Brontë, ISBN: 9788193545898
- Your Faith is Your Fortune by Neville Goddard, ISBN: 9789389157161
- Zen in the Art of Archery by Eugen Herrigel, ISBN: 9789354991059

Develop your reading habit | **Gift books to your friends**

www.ingramcontent.com/pod-product-compliance
Ingram Content Group UK Ltd.
Pitfield, Milton Keynes, MK11 3LW, UK
UKHW032042260826
14628UKWH00008B/3129

9 789354 993800